ENZIO'S KINGDOM

AND OTHER POEMS

BY

WILLIAM ALEXANDER PERCY

Copyright © 2013 Read Books Ltd.
This book is copyright and may not be
reproduced or copied in any way without
the express permission of the publisher in writing

British Library Cataloguing-in-Publication Data
A catalogue record for this book is available from the
British Library

William Alexander Percy

William Alexander Percy was born on 14 May, 1885 in Greenville, Mississippi, USA. His mother, Camille, was a strong French Catholic, and his father, LeRoy Percy was the last United States Senator from Mississippi, elected by legislature. The family were very influential in the state, owning 20,000 acres of cotton plantation, and Percy used this influence to champion his mother's Catholic religion in an overwhelmingly Protestant area. As a young man, Percy travelled to Paris before reading law at *Harvard University*. He joined his father's law firm after graduating. During the First World War, Percy served in Belgium as a delegate to the *Commission for Relief in Belgium*, and remained there until America declared war in 1917. Thereafter, Percy served in the US army, earning the rank of Captain and was awarded the *Croix de Guerre* for his bravery. On returning from the war, Percy edited the *Yale Younger Poets* series (until 1932) and also published four further volumes of poetry with the *Yale University Press*. It was here that he befriended many members of the contemporary literary elite as well as several members of the *Harlem Renaissance,* a movement which promoted African-American cultural expression. Having known Herbert Hoover from his time in the *Belgium Relief Effort*, Percy was placed in charge of relief during the great flood of 1927. He was incredibly concerned about the poor conditions, healthcare and nutrition offered to the mainly black refugees fleeing flooded farms and plantations across Mississippi. Percy believed that the people needed to be evacuated to nearby Vicksburg in Warren County to ensure their health and wellbeing. However after several local planters, including Percy's own father, opposed the decision, conditions for the refugees deteriorated severely and Percy was strongly criticised in the national press. After this debacle, he soon resigned. Percy is best known for his memoir, *Lanterns on the Levee: Recollections of a Planter's Son*, published in 1941, but he also wrote poetry, published in *Collected Poems* (1943) and the text of *They Cast Their Nets in Galilee*, included in the *Episcopal Hymnal* (1982). He died on 21 January, 1954, at the age of 69.

IN MEMORY OF MY FRIEND
CAROLINE STERN
THE POET
TO WHOM I AM MOST INDEBTED

TABLE OF CONTENTS

Lyrics: PAGE

October 3
A Canticle 4
To One Dying 7
Courage 8
His Peace 9
Hymn of the Magdalene 10
Beth Marie 11
Autumn Song 12
For a Word 13
Safe Secrets 14
Youth 15
Sight and Sound 16
She Grieves in the Dusk 17
Afterglow 18
The Unloved to his Belovèd 19
A Mad Maid's Song 20
Exchange 21
A Debussy Serenade 22
Winds of Winter 23
Hymn to the Sun 24
Compensation 25
That Kingdom 26
Autumn Wisdom 27
One Path 29
To a Stranger 30
Wonder and a Thousand Springs 31
Calypso to Ulysses 32

	PAGE
Spring Night in the Mountains	34
Siren Song	35
A Letter	37
After Hearing Music	38
In the Cold Bright Wind	39
The Green Bird Seeth Iseult	40
Avernel	42
Canopus	43
French Blue	45
For a Poet's Birthday	46
A Portrait	47
Rain Patter	48
Meditating a Journey	50
Italian Summer	51
Delight	52
Advice in Springtime	53
Insomnia	54
Sublimation	55
Four Capri Impromptus	56
An Arcadian Idyll	59
A Brittany Idyll	62

DELTA SKETCHES:

In the Delta	71
Greenville Trees	
The Lombardy Poplars	73
The China-Berries	73
The Locusts	75
The Water Oaks	76
The Holy Women	79
A Burnished Calm	80

TABLE OF CONTENTS

	PAGE
Levee Nocturne	81
A Memory	82
Song	84
Outcast	85
The Delta Autumn	86
A Letter from John Keats to Fanny Brawne	89
Enzio's Kingdom	99
Epilogue	140

LYRICS

*Diverging paths we climb,
But if you find a flower
I will applaud its perfume,
I will confess its power.*

*I seek an amaranth
More lovely than its name,
For me a very heart's rue,
For your hearts not the same.*

*It blows above the blue
Far-vistaed Paphian sea,
Or so the woman said
Whose green eyes 'sorcelled me.*

*Joy to you in your meadows,
But I'll search mine alone
And find an amaranth—
Or else a quiet stone.*

OCTOBER

THESE are the days, too few, that I would hold
Of birds that pause before they seek the south,
Of leaves that rustle not, but, dying, fall
In richer beauty than they ever lived,

Of light that is too merciful at last
To be all gold, but aureoles with blue
Or such dim purple as the moon exhales
The wasted brambles and the wounded trees.

Now are untended ways made beautiful
By cobweb flowers, the wistfullest I know,
Rememberers of all forgotten dead—
Wild asters in my country they are called.

At last it is too late for all regret,
Too late for deeds, and dreams hold no reproach,
And might have been is vague as what may be,
And all is well though much has never been.

A CANTICLE

LOVELY is daytime when the joyful sun goes singing,
Lovely is night with stars and round or sickled moon,
Lovely are trees, forever lovely, whether in winter
Or musical midsummer or when they bud and tassel
Or crown themselves with stormy splendors in the fall.
But lovelier than day or night or trees in blossom
Is there no secret infinite loveliness behind?

Beautiful is water, running on rocks in mountains,
Or bosoming sunsets where the valley rivers ponder;
Beautiful is ocean with its myriad colors,
Its southern blues and purples, its arctic gray and silver,
Blown into green frost-fretted or wine-dark in the evening.
But still more beautiful than waters calm or cloven,
Than ocean thunder-maned or floored for delicate springtime,
Is there no beauty visible save to our eyes?

Marvellous is the grass, friendly and very clean,
Though intimate with all the dead, the ceaseless dead,
It has great heart and makes the ancient earth forgetful;
It is not troubled by the wind and from the storm
It learns a radiance; all night it wears the dew
And in the morning it is glad with a pure gladness.

A CANTICLE

More marvellous than dew-strown morning grasses, is there
No brave immortal joyousness that wrought the grass?

Who lifteth in the eastern sky the dark, gold moon?
Who painteth green and purple on the blackbird's throat?
What hand of rapture scattereth sunshine through the rain
And flingeth round the barren boughs of spring returned
Dim fire? Who stenciled with caught breath the moth's wide wing
And lit the ruby in his eyes? Whose ecstasy
Set silver ripples on the racing thunder-cloud
And flared the walls of storm with terrible dead green?
What dreamer fretted dew upon the flat-leafed corn
And twined in innocence of useless perfect art
The morning-glory with its bubble blue, soon gone?
Was there no hand that braided autumn branches in
Their solemn brede and stained them with a sombre rust?
Was there no love conceived the one-starred, rivered evening,
And dipped in crocus fire the gray horns of the moon?

They say there never was a god men loved but died—
Dead is Astarte, Astoreth is dead, and Baal;
Zeus and Jehovah share a single grave and deep;
Olympus hears no laughter, Sinai no voice;
Spring comes, but Freia comes not nor Persephone:
On temple plinth and porch the random grasses run;

ENZIO'S KINGDOM

Of all their priests alone the white-stoled stars are
    faithful.
Dead are the gods, forever dead! And yet—and yet—
Who lifteth in the eastern sky the dark, gold moon? ...
There is a loveliness outlasts the temporal gods,
A beauty that, when all we know as beautiful
Is gone, will fashion in delight the forms it loves,
In that wide room where all our stars are but a drift
Of glimmering petals down an air from far away.

TO ONE DYING

WHEN you are gone the stars will be content,
Gazing as always in the deep of ocean;
There will not be a fluttering bird that cries
With anguish more importunate beneath the moon;
The rolling seasons with unhindered flow
Of bloom and scarlet tatterings and feathered ice
Will fold the world in loveliness as now.
But I shall have but these, and these with glory shorn
And half invisible because you went. . . .
Then I shall pass. And none because of me
Will be less glad of spring or watch with eyes that blur
The evening's one bright star.
Only, I think, in some remote demesne
That you have learned to love regretfully
There will be added brightness and a cry
Of patient waiting done.

COURAGE

INTO a brown wood flew a brown bird
  In the winter time:
The sky was dark with snow unfallen,
  The leaves were bent with rime.

Once north he flew, once south he flew,
  He perched in a naked tree.
He looked into the dismal dusk
  And whistled merrily.

HIS PEACE

I LOVE to think of them at dawn
Beneath the frail pink sky
Casting their nets in Galilee
And fish-hawks circling by.

Casting their nets in Galilee
Just off the hills of brown,
Such happy, simple fisherfolk
Before the Lord walked down.

Contented, peaceful fishermen,
Before they ever knew
The peace of God that filled their hearts
Brim-full, and broke them too.

Young John who trimmed the flapping sail,
Homeless, in Patmos died.
Peter who hauled the teeming net,
Head-down, was crucified.

The peace of God, it is no peace,
But strife closed in the sod.
Yet, brothers, pray for but one thing,
The marvellous peace of God.

HYMN OF THE MAGDALENE

I COULD not see the morning stars He made,
Nor hear the morning birds who pray aloud;
The flowers were not my brothers nor the winds
Who blow the silver-linèd trees to cloud.

No light upon the hills, no purple bloom
Behind the lifting moon in summer time;
No sweetness in the everyday of life,
No peace, no tears, no rest in Fancy's clime.

But now my sin is done and I can lift
Mine eyes unto the mansions that He made,
And I am wrapped about with holiness
And drenched in glories that can never fade.

Yea, I have put mine olden sin away
And broke and strewn my heart beneath His feet;
His wisdom robbeth me of any fear,
His tenderness upon my mouth is sweet.

O holy light upon the sacred hills,
O birds that flash above the flowered sod,
O clean, immortal beauty of the earth,
I have returned to you and to my God!

BETH MARIE

IMPATIENTLY she drew her breath,
  So new was life, so wild:
But patiently she waited death
  And when he touched her, smiled.

She who had never wished to die,
  Who had such fear of pain,
Was tranquil as an evening sky
  That flowers from spent rain.

For us her loss was different
  From all we could suppose:
The calm of Spartan stars she lent
  Who only seemed a rose.

AUTUMN SONG

TIME was when billowy autumn skies
   And red rain-dabbled leaves
Would fling the tears across my eyes.
   'Tis happiness that grieves.

Now lengths of scarlet-littered rain
   May lash the howling eaves;
My eyes are casual as pain.
   'Tis happiness that grieves.

FOR A WORD

How shall you ever know the adoration
I spread like samite cloths beneath your feet?
How shall you guess the brooding desolation
Learned from your eyes so passionless and sweet?

There must be some word like the star that pauses
In summer's rose transparency of dusk,
Or like the bird-note heard through slumber's gauzes
The unsilvering hour before dew warms to musk.

There must be some one word that is more tender
Than any word my lips have ever learned,
Without which I can never, never render
In speech the love your cool sweet love has earned.

You know as none my heart's forlorn distresses,
Its passionate tides, its daily tint and glow,—
Why must there be within obscure recesses
This tenderness of love you cannot know?

SAFE SECRETS

I WILL carry terrible things to the grave with me:
  So much must never be told.
My eyes will be ready for sleep and my heart for dust
  With all the secrets they hold.
The piteous things alive in my memory
  Will be safe in that soundless dwelling:
In the clean loam, in the dark where the dumb roots rust
  I can sleep without fear of telling.

YOUTH

When I look on the youth of the world I weep:
Their eyes are so shadowless and candid,
They run so eagerly to meet the future,
They are so beautiful even in their passions—
So restless to live, so fickle, so yearning;
They have such faith in happiness,
Such songs in their hearts, such dreams in their eyes.
The light of them shines like light on the meadows,
Their laughter is sturdy and full of innocence;
Their vehemence, their proud assurance,
And most, their sweetness and their happiness
I watch till my eyes are blurred with pity.
For they will learn and wither with their learning;
Their flower look will die a flower's death.
And one will learn of love and one of want
And one of death and one of weakened will,
But all will learn and all will weep alone.
There will be no shining left for death to darken,
And their lovely throats and eyes will not be lovely
Before the dust corrodes them, long before.
Cold pain will kiss them and they will not smile
As once they smiled when peach-blow kisses fell;
And fear will blanch the red run of their blood,
And doubt uncurve the bow of their sweet mouths,
And tears that were a gust of gold-shot rain
Will turn a brackish drink for their poor hearts,
And they will know what we have known too long.
Spare them, O heartless gods who spared not us!

SIGHT AND SOUND

I saw a handful of white stars
Blooming in a width of grass;
I saw a cherry tree, snow-white,
In woods as naked-cold as glass.

I saw a blue leaf zigzag down—
The bluebird with his russet throat!
From out the sallow cane-brake stole
Another bluebird's aching note.

The blue, the white, I wrote them down
To soothe my heart when spring was over.
No need, or help, alas, to write
That bluebird's "Lover, lover, lover!"

SHE GRIEVES IN THE DUSK

Ah, he was white and slender
And the lamplight turned him gold
And his groping hands were tender
And his kisses never bold.
How shall I sleep through the long, long nights
In my wide cold-sheeted bed,
Hearing the wild geese crying in their flights,
And me afraid,
And him not by to turn and hold me to his heart
In the way he knew,
And me no longer folded to his heart,
Thinking him true!

AFTERGLOW

Limpid lavender like water-hyacinths
The light floods on after the sun is down
And tips ethereally the primrose moon.
There is a delicate music in the films of the air,
And I remember how I saw, long, long ago,
A primrose slip of a girl, with lowered lids
And fugitive smile such as Luini loved,
Flush ethereally with the flooding of first love.

THE UNLOVED TO HIS BELOVED

Could I pluck down Aldebaran
And haze the Pleiads in your hair
I could not add more burning to your beauty
Or lend a starrier coldness to your air.

If I were cleaving terrible waters
With death ahead on the visible sands
I could not turn and stretch my hands more wildly,
More vainly turn and stretch to you my hands.

A MAD MAID'S SONG

Here's tansy for you, and a sprig of rue.
Such simples are not worn upon the brow,
   But next a heart they'll keep it true—
      Or did till now.
A sprig of rue should keep it true
And tansy's good as any vow.
But round your heart, not round your brow
Wear them, and wear enough for two.

EXCHANGE

It does not seem a piteous thing to pass
From out the passionate sunlight and to never see
   Light-loving winds press down the tremulous grass
      Inconstantly.

The closing of the eyes, the clean forgetting,
The silence broken by no whispering love-calls,
   These willingly I'd take—not once regretting
      Unheard footfalls.

What power lies in long, untender kisses
To steal the tears from pain, the innocence from mirth!
   What loved exchange—these desolate, hurt blisses
      For folded earth!

A DEBUSSY SERENADE

Love, they say, is kind:
    Nay, wrinkles here
And here love gave to me
    And quenched my eyes.
    Love is not kind.

A god, they say, is love.
    Do gods, then, dull
The aureate dawn and bleach
    The purple haze?
    No god is love.

A boy, they say, is love.
    His hunter's eyes,
Alert and cold, I saw,
    Insatiable,
    And they were old.

Give back, O love, give back
    What you have stole,
And I will make return
    Of all your gifts—
    And go, enriched.

WINDS OF WINTER

SHAKE out, dark-tressed and multitudinous storm-winds,
Your theft of scarlet leaves for Hecate's hair,
Your coral bits from autumn's dead clenched hand,
Your brittle blooms that once had breath and color,
Asters and docks and hateful immortelles—
Scatter them down, but bear away the summer
And hopes that were and loves that could not be.
Strip off the garlands, hang the trees with fire
Of frost and clanking armor of blue ice.
There is much death abroad and for a tomb
Starkness were needed and unmelted tears.
Welcome, dark-tressed and multitudinous storm-winds.

HYMN TO THE SUN

STRIKE down into my breast, O sun, and cleanse my
    soul—
Shadows are here and ailments of the dark!
Burn out the horror, sear away the dread,
Beat like live hope in spark on molten spark.

Lone in your uncouth solitude of chasmed air
You scale the sky, reckless of end or change,
Chanting like some wild Himalayan shepherd
Wind-rocked, enraptured, on his bleak vast range.

Eternity will pass and down the blue cliffs hear
You singing, vigorous still in fierce delight.
Strike through my breast and pour your courage
    in—
Enough to last this little way to night.

COMPENSATION

Delicious hurt is in the throb
Of every ruby in youth's blood:
Moonlight or love can call a sob,
Or red trees in a drizzling wood.

We own a strength we never guess
When warm and weak with April's wine,
A fortitude against the stress
Of tragic things young hearts divine.

The visions that we could not bear
Turned facts are borne almost with grace:
The future with its heartbreak air
Arrives unflushed and commonplace.

Far-travelled in the land of pain,
Fate's clear worst warrant learned by rote,
I watch the red trees in the rain
With eyes undimmed and unhurt throat.

THAT KINGDOM

FINGERLESS cactus hands heal in the sun
And tortured olive trees grope up the hills;
A lizard feigns to sleep but flinching kills
The busy spider in her web half done.

The gaunt Sicilian pastures burn blue-white,
The sunlight rains its blue perpetual rain;
The south is still the south, but not again
Shall I find there my kingdom, Heart's Delight.

Oh, not on hills of blue eternal lustre
Build we the kingdom of our heart's delight,
But on love's shale, that quakes above a night
Where ocean yawns and screaming storm-birds cluster.

AUTUMN WISDOM

THE nights of autumn stars are never still,
For without gust the heavy acorns fall
And rattle on the roof—the oak's proud gift
And happy show of his accomplishment.

For this he shouldered storms and stripping hail,
For this unwrinkled in the weak spring sun
His velvet buds and shook his tassels out
And ruffled noisily in boisterous May.

For this—a fall of acorns in the starlight.
But where they fall, what burgeoning or death
Awaits them on the sparkling, plangent ground
Are not to his bronze peace inquietudes.

On glittering shale, perhaps, or sterile sand
Their hope of swelling spring will waste away;
Perhaps the droves of night-marauding hogs,
Scuffling and loud, will eat the last smooth one;

Perhaps the little children, up at dawn,
Scouring the deep-rimed leaves for treasure-trove,
Will set them with their spools and broken glass
For patterns in their fairy palaces;

Perhaps not one will burst and branch and grow
A windy place for elf-eyed boys to climb,
A shade for clasping lovers in the night,
A spangled roof for old folk in the rain.

He will not care: his joy is to have done
The appointed deed, not guess the deed's result.
Along his branches creeps the bright-eyed frost.
He spills his fruit and laughs against the stars.

ONE PATH

OUTSIDE the Earthly Paradise,
    Beneath its cool high walls,
I walk the little grass-blurred path
    Where sunlight seldom falls.

I try no more the guarded gates
    That will not let me in;
I cease to wonder what the cause,
    What accident, what sin.

I walk the lonely path that's mine,
    My heart and I employ
Our solitude in songs about
    The near-by Kingdom's joy.

And once, while singing thus, we heard
    Applause and friendly cries,
And saw, high up, our happy kin,
    Love in their lovely eyes.

The path of lonely wayfaring
    Ends where I cannot tell:
Outside the Earthly Paradise
    I know—but that is well.

TO A STRANGER

When I see your beauty the beasts in me lie down
And I know the good man that I might have been.
To watch you is more cleansing than clear sunsets
And more regretful than the deeds that I have done.
If memory could only keep me perfect
And not fade out to leave me with myself!
With all my altars ashes and my gods asleep
You with your marvellous sad infinite beauty
Make me kneel down and know what life could be—
Unhurtfulness and worship and sure trust.
But I have missed you in the passing of the ships
And as a stranger only watch you pass.
Yet seeing you tonight in your great beauty
I shall dream calmly of a clear green sky
Filled with wild white swans flying, flying over,
Against the hardly-visible, wide-swarming stars.

WONDER AND A THOUSAND SPRINGS

ALONG the just-returning green
That fledges field and berm and brake
The purple-veined white violets lean,
    Scarcely awake;

And pear and plum and apple trees,
Evoked to bloom before they leaf,
Lift cloudy branches filled with bees
    Strange as new grief.

A thousand springs will poise and pass
And leave no track beneath the sun:
Some gray-eyed lad, cool-cheeked as grass,
    Will watch each one,

And wonder, as I wonder here,
And find no clue I have not found,
And smile before he joins me, near
    But underground.

CALYPSO TO ULYSSES

If there were any room within my heart
For godly pride to linger, I should not kneel
And clasp your feet. But there's no tenant here
Save love, and he has made me your idolater.

I am alone, belovèd, but for you.
Cast out the sea-look from your eyes and look
On me, my utter self—no luring left,
No unused wile to whet your appetite.

You know me all, and all of me is yours.
I should have kept some harlot reticence
To bate the surfeiting beast in you. Alas!
Shrink not. Men's modesty is but in speech.

These are still gray eyes and pomegranate lips
As once you called them, whispering through my hair
In the dawn-stillness when the dawn-bird sang,
And blissfully your drowsy kisses clung.

What is the loss that loses me your favor,
Your misty voice, your eyes spilled full of color,
Your hands whose very stillness in a curve
Betrayed their greediness to reach for mine?

Ah, do you dream, lover no longer young,
That those frail ecstasies can be lived over
If only on some new young breast you slumber
And fresher lips yearn to you in the dark?

ENZIO'S KINGDOM

There is no second spring: your first is past
And it was passed with me and you are mine!
Or can a woman never claim as hers
The heart of any man before it breaks?

Oh, is the love of man a sunset waning,
A music slipping by, a one day's flower,
Its very fleetingness the magic flaw
That lures the fixed idolatrous love of woman?

Say not it is the sea that summons you,
Or such affairs as chafing heroes plan:
Hearted as that fierce pleading wanderer
That once was you, nothing could draw you from me!

Belovèd, leave me not! There is such terror
In the loneliness of souls that once were large!
Though yours be never lonely, without you
Mine were a gray rock in a wintry sun.

No use, no use! The touch of you tells me that.
This body that I gave you when the gift
Was begged as sole alternative to death
Has served and staled. . . . The sea calls and you go.

Then go. . . . No, I should hate a sea-cold kiss;
Remembered ones will do. . . . And I'll endure
Loneliness with more profit and more pride
Than you an aging man's concupiscence.

SPRING NIGHT IN THE MOUNTAINS

THE lakes of the sky are clearer than day
    And all but the great stars are drowned,
The glorying winds and the phosphorous clouds
    Fling the dark in swift coils on the ground,
And the burning bleared moon in a halo of bronze
    Is dashed through the zenith like sound.

It should be cold when the trees are so bare
    Or the breezes spring-gentled for flight,
Not torturing thus the dogwood that writhes
    Like a desperate immaculate light.
I am afraid of the night and the spring
    And the terrible winds of the night!

Afraid of the rapture that grapples and tears
    Till the cords of my heart are torn,
While the moonlight is crashing down canyons of cloud
    Like blasts from a great silver horn,
And all the impenitent lovers, long dead,
    Are blown past, lip to lip, unforsworn.

SIREN SONG

THESE are the seaward cliffs: let us sing and forget.
The daylight dazzles upon us, cloudless and clean,
And there, far down, where the crimson rocks are wet,
Shallows mottle the sapphire sea with green.
    Come, let us forget,
And, healed of ancient tears and whole of ancient teen,
    Sing with cold hearts of joy and no regret.

Fair from safe hill-tops seem the passing sails,
Fairer perhaps because they always pass,
And that far mountain-land, that quakes and pales
In the noon stillness, fair too and far, alas!
    No rough sweet hails
Will glitter up our glens, nor will a bruised bright grass
    Betray some parting's anguish in our vales.

We are accursed. Why should our thoughts yet cling
To them that loved us when they knew us not,
But learning us despised? Come, let us sing
Forgetfully, loving this lovely spot
    Where the swallows swing
Half down the cliff white-breasted, shrill, and the haze is hot
    Plumbago blue like a witch's eyes in spring.

Not the wind's fingers scribbling on the floor
Of ocean write a rune more incomplete

And mad than that fate marked above the door
Of our strange hearts, set open to all feet.
      Oh, seek no more
Its meaning. Sing, let our songs be ignorantly sweet
    Like upland waters pluming as they pour.

Alas! no music sounds here save our tears
And all things we have won except forgetfulness!
      Our longing veers
    Back to the native land of our distress—
      No sights may bless
Eyes the red needle of endurance sears.
Then let us sing again with heartbreak wise and mad
The terrible songs we sang once ere we came,
And win the round windy ocean that was glad
To be one sorrowing echo of our shame.
    Never, never, never may we unlearn
    The secret with which we burn,
      Never appease
    Our mortal hurt with these
      Felicities.
      Again
    Lift we our voices,
Our music old with bitterness and bane,
For we weave our songs and our songs are woven
      Of pain,
And the heart that sings is the heart that is cloven.

A LETTER

AID my heart in its fidelity!
Though my unfaith were no regret to you
It would betray, O careless heart I love,
Not only you, but love itself, and me.
That I am absent brings no pain to you,
But every hour away is death to me—
Send me some word, though heartless as your love,
And aid my heart in its fidelity.

AFTER HEARING MUSIC

Give me a breath of air!
There is too much of sweetness here,
Too much of pain, pain blent with loveliness.
I am allured from all that we call living
And sickened of the harsh necessities.
The earth again! the earth where sweat is poured
To rise in bronze ripe undulant fields of grain,
Where here and now is sinewed hardihood
And intertwining effort vain and vast.
What now is Avalon, or purple ships that plow
The dim blue evening full of mists and tears?
Give me a breath of air, a sound of voices,
For I am drugged with dreams
And smothered with the smoke of old disasters.
Of what avail dead lovers laid in Avalon
Or purple ships outbound?

IN THE COLD BRIGHT WIND

MERLIN, Merlin's gone away
   With a limmer witch for spouse,
He's gone to spend a sorry year
   In the Queen o' Fairies' house.

For gear he's took the sapphire bird
   Wi' the bubble in his throat;
His hat was prinked wi' the wee wet flowers
   That gaud daft April's coat.

Sunny-cold the bold wind blew
   As he strode off down the hill;
His red cloak bellied out and swirled,
   His eyes burned gray and chill.

For promise of a warm high bed
   And spiced renewing drink
He's footed it to Fairyland
   Where love's the only swink.

He's gone away, and not alone—
   Brightly, oh, he sinned!
His red cloak glimmers on the thorn
   And his laughter on the wind.

THE GREEN BIRD SEETH ISEULT

A GREEN bird on a golden bush,
    And the leaves chimed out and spake:
"What have you seen, what heard, green bird,
    Since you heard the blue day break?"

"A sea, a sea, a saffron sea,
    And a creamy warm full sail
Floating beneath me as I flew,
    And my shadow stamped the sail
Like a clover leaf, a green clover leaf,
    Blown from an Irish dale."

"Did lovers pale stand by the sail
    That furrowed the Irish sea?
Did you catch the glimmer of golden mail
    And the glimmer of hair blown free?"

"Golden each scale of his burnished mail
    And her hair was bronze and gold:
From an emerald cup I saw them sup
    That their four hands scarce could hold."

"Delight and woe, delight and woe,
    Bird of the Irish sea—
These they drank up from the emerald cup
    On the sun-swooned saffron sea."

THE GREEN BIRD SEETH ISEULT

"Only delight, only delight,
While the beautiful burning blue daylight
    Was dappled by me
With the green leaf-shadow shapen in three.
Delight I saw, delight I heard!"
Sang the sunlight-aureoled emerald bird
    To the golden tree
      Deliriously.

AVERNEL

From Avernel the hills flow down
    And leave it near the sky,
And it has birds and bells and trees
    And fauns that never die.

When coral-pink azaleas fill
    Its roomy woods with sweet,
And lilac spills of violets wait
    For violet-veined swift feet;

When moths are budded by the oaks'
    Uncrinkling rose and red
And high, high up, green butterflies
    Reveal the poplars' head;

When shaggy clouds in single bliss
    Blaze up the sea-blue air,
Spilling their shadow-amethyst
    Along the hills' wide stair;

Then there is singing in the sun
    And whispering in the shade
And dancing till the stars slope down
    Their murmurous arcade.

In love's half sleep the curly faun's
    Uncertain if he sees
Orion or first fireflies
    Between the clear dark trees.

CANOPUS

When February brings the hopeless days
And there's no cranny of the silent world
Where grass is green or boughs are fresh
Or birds recall their litanies of love,
And earth seems but a place where graves are dug
And dug too tardily—
Then turn for peace to those forgotten stars
That change not with the changes of the year,
But still pursue their purposed ministries
In the cold night,
Though loveliness lies dead upon the ground.
Then their serene proud ranks receive
From thick-starred equatorial climes
A lone and flaming guest,
The lord and love of all the southern sky.
Above, aye, just above the black horizon
When the first dark is clear,
You see him rise, superb and alien,
The fiery-haired Canopus, surging from the south.
But one vast scornful stare he flings
Across the full curve of the northern night
Wherein Arcturus and Aldebaran
Marshal the bright-helmed sons of heaven;
Then, meeting the blue gaze of Sirius,
Turns, and retreating down the crystal dark
Hides from our eyes his haughty slow return.
The serpentining Amazon
And many a lost lagoon, flamingo-stirred,

Mirror his golden shaggy hair;
The wide-palmed plantain-leaves
Receive in sleep his tread,
And glimmer, dreaming that the moon glows past;
In their rough pastures
Bronze Peruvian shepherds mark his course
And call his name, and vainly call.
For he strides on in his dim godly wrath
Past Ecuador
And the long samite carpet of the Argentine,
Past the incredible drear rooms of stone
The Incas built, by night, to helpless gods,
On precipices of the fearful Andes;
Nor stays his step till he descries, far down,
The ghostly mountainous antipodes,
Mute with blue cold.
There, trembling in his wreath of flames, he halts
And gazes on the glistering nether pole
Where his reflection shakes—
Contemplative
And sunk in his own thought.
But then our land is gay with polished leaves
And birds are nesting in the calm sweet sun.

FRENCH BLUE

THERE'S a blue flower grows in France,
    A tattered roadside thing,
Like flowers cut, by little girls,
    Of paper while they sing,

Which when I see so far from home
    I feel tears almost rise,
For it is blue with just the blue
    Of one dear lady's eyes.

FOR A POET'S BIRTHDAY

THE plowman breaks the smelling earth
   And birds are in his wake;
He scatters seed for harvesting,
   They, song for singing's sake.

His heedful heart is happy as
   Their hearts that take no heed—
But happiest the furrow's heart
   Where song is sown with seed.

A PORTRAIT

When I see you I think of Mary, the mother of God,
Before she was a mother. But you are older,
Though young, so young that when I think of Calvary
I do not see you fainting at the cross
But bending over her who faints, your arms
About her, your tears upon her face, your voice
Comforting, were there comfort in the world.
Yet there's no beauty of the sweet-aired earth
Not reminiscent to my heart of you:
Water, the very pure winds of heaven, and the dew,
Birds at their matins, all limpid-colored flowers,
Not those that blaze in peacock opulence,
But such compassionate and candid blooms
As hurt the throat: branches of half-blushed peach,
Anemones that have a just-born air,
Miraculous, blue, breathless morning-glories,
Crocuses far too cool to be like flames,
And cosmos only of the autumn host.
These certainly I know to be your kin.
Yet this, your outward self, could dull and tarnish
And still your loveliness would be no less
And still men could not fail to see in you
That which they always hope to find in women—
The unnameable gay goodness that they love,
Attained in tears, most evident in smiles,
And more worth dying for than creed or crown. . . .
No wonder, seeing you, I think of Mary,
The mother of God, before she was a mother.

RAIN PATTER

The lambs are sleeping in the rain
Cuddled two and two together,
One alone might sleep in pain
On the hillside in such weather.
In the spring rain slow and steady,
Just before the leaves are ready,
Walking is contentment's gain,
That is, walking with another,
Best a lover, then heart's brother—
All alone might waken pain.
Come then, dear, be wise again,
Ramble with me in the soft spring rain—
Walking is contentment's gain!
We'll see weeping willow's mane
Beaded with the moonstone rain,
Then the oat-field's emerald stain,
Then a brambled dripping lane
Where johnny-jump-ups, pert and plain,
Are common as the inch-high grain.
If walking's more than going's art
Unaided by curt car or cart,
Your eyes a thief, a sleuth your heart,
We'll find, I have no doubt at all,
Right in the cold wood's hollow cove
Branches of blurry pink I love—
(The red-bud always has his anguish out
Before the leaves are there to laugh and flout).
We'll surely see a redbird fall

RAIN PATTER

And hear, if you'll not breathe at all,
The tentative self-conscious call
Of the young mockingbird who slyly
Practises what he sings not shyly
At windows and from garden borders
When what he sings is what he orders.
(But men have lived and died quite near
And never heard his muted fear,
So exquisite and faint and clear.)
What if I should show to you
A plum tree and a cherry too,
Both white as lilies Mary grew,
And hazed about with rain?
Oh, if we go as I like best,
Haphazardly and with a zest,
You'll have no need to seek for pleasure
In lands that other daytimes measure,
But every bush will be your treasure!
Come out, come out, be wise again
Before the spring begins to wane—
There's nothing gladder, I maintain,
Than walking together in the rain!

MEDITATING A JOURNEY

The swallows curling in the sky,
Less wishful to be gone than I,
Well know the land whereto they fly
    In fickle flight.
To bathe in sun-soothed southern air,
Where one cloud-shadow is as rare
As true love, is their only care
    And sole delight.
But I, what south could I attain
That would not seem a journey vain
When all my sun doth here remain,
    How coldly bright!

ITALIAN SUMMER

TIBERIUS is in his grave,
But where that is who's saying?
It's long and long since hereabouts
Poppaea went a-maying.

Oh, all the hearts that on this breeze
Brush by like motes of gold!
The many a tear, the many a kiss
No secret to this mold!

Oh, let's not let the lovely dead
Distract us from our passion—
They are so dead, so soon we'll be!
Love passes like a fashion.

Palazzo di Tiberio.

DELIGHT

Delight it is has kept me
From thinking much, I fear,
And I'd have loved more wisely
Had not delight been near;
And tears a few he's cost me,
But saved me many a tear.

O friends that I have clung to
To save me from time's spite,
O loves of mine whom kissing
I've wished all time were night—
I'd keep you all, but lose you
Before I'd lose delight!

ADVICE IN SPRINGTIME

When evening skies are smoked with rose,
And dubious spring behind the hill
To come or not a thistle blows,
And buds amaze wet puckered snows—
Then watch your will, your lazy will,
For then he loves to sleep his fill.

He yawns if yearning's in the breeze,
Nods at violets paused before,
And should you watch with soft unease
The sad blood-pink of Judas trees,
He's sleeping sure, content to snore
At warm temptation's very door.

To nunneries, you maidens all!
You old despairs of saving grace,
Young men so lusty-limbed and tall,
To desert caves and diets small!
For earth's a shameful, sighful place
Beneath the unwimpled spring's embrace.

INSOMNIA

O LITTLE boats of Capri
That fish a mile from town
And nick the dark with torches
Till heaven is upside-down,

I may forget these brown warm eyes,
These brown throats as they turn,
These girls with burdens on their heads
Like Greek girls on an urn;

Their dark-lashed, rascal sweetness,
Their smiles I may forget,—
But not your constellations
Splashed gold on miles of jet.

Above you Mars and Spica
Curve down into the sea,
Springing from you the Scorpion's vine
Festoons the heavenly tree.

May all your nets be silver-chocked,
May all your sails win through!
In each of you were sleepless eyes
When mine were sleepless, too.

SUBLIMATION

Lock your sin in a willow cage,
　Cover the key with clay:
Hanging beneath your rafters' shade
　He'll sing for you some day.

Outside your good deeds cluck and strut,
　But small's the joy they bring.
It's only a wistful prisoner bird
　With a wicked heart can sing.

Break not the lock, bend not the withes!
　Escaping through some chink,
His song will cease—in your live heart
　His beak will take its drink.

FOUR CAPRI IMPROMPTUS

I.

Sweet as the furze flower fainting in the noon heat,
The yellow furze flower tufted in a cliff above the
    ocean,
Floating its too sweet perfume over the peacock waters
And weakening the diving swallows half down the
    air—
So sweet, so weakening the breath of you comes to me,
    belovèd,
When I lean over you, or even, even when I dream of
    you, my flower.

II.

Mournful and miraculous beauty bathes the sea
When the rose-misted sun melts out,
And for one perfect moment—
While two swallows can eddy and plunge their white
    breasts
From the cliff-crest to the beach—
The waters are misty rose for infinite miles
Save for the silver chariot-tracks of the winds;
Curving and leading nowhere and always silver,
But edged, how strangely, with keen victorious green.

III.

Just over the gray cliffs
In the blue brumal air
Glistens a faint unwilling Hesper,

FOUR CAPRI IMPROMPTUS

His curls bound with a fillet of white fire.
Along the sky his steps seem slow
Like a young sulky god's,
So I should see him as he stands a moment
Dreamily on the cliff top, between the two twisted stone-pines.
There he may pause and watch the blue lilies of the twilight
Like sleep-flowers on the fields of the still sea,
Blue-gray like sleep-flowers on the mountain flanks
And the coves of the unwindy coming night.
There I have stood on other evenings
Watching a long time the lonely twilight.
But the young Hesper has no heart to look.
Barely I saw his silver instep touch the top
And he was gone—
Running, running, not pausing for a glance,
Down the dark other side of the sheep-strewn cliff.
He is no shepherd:
He had no tawny wisp of net over his arm,
No net to cast in the foam-flowered breakers from the beach
Like a fisher-boy.
I think he has some love far down on the tilted side in the darkness
To whom he hurries—
A nymph perhaps, maybe another star
With floating hair and a girl's silver body.
Surely with such a single amorous haste
Before the night is over,
Even before the Pleiads tremble up,
He will be with her,

ENZIO'S KINGDOM

Lying, I dare say, greedily,
The sweat-beads pearling still the curve of his shoulders
And his breast still heaving.

IV.

I shall bring you blue morning-glories ribbed with purple,
Or hazy-blue plumbago flowers.
But they will not please you: they have no perfume.
Shall I search higher and twitch a spray of golden gorse?
The bees cannot leave it
And it is sweeter and more golden than their honey.
Or I know a cleft above the sapphire ocean
Where grows one shoot of the wild oleander.
Its flowers are crimson pink:
Some say it is Adonis' blood that they are dipped in,
Others, more rightly, Aphrodite's own.
And their perfume when full open in the noon heats
Has often made a passing dryad drowsy.
Pan never nears their shadow except on tiptoe—
He has made lucky finds in their sleepy shade.
But you—none of these will content you,
Neither the blue morning-glories
Nor ash-blue clusters of plumbago
Nor gorse that is golden yellow
Nor blood-rose oleanders.
How shall I hope that my heart may please you
Which is less lovely than these,
But not less quickly withered?

AN ARCADIAN IDYLL

Far, far from here,
Above Andritsaena,
In the naked hills that paling darkness covers,
A sandalled goatherd climbs the path
Behind his flock.
Vacant the sleeping pastures,
For the bees, too, still are sleeping,
Vacant and thick with dew and flower-strown,
Tempting to bearded goats.
Slowly he follows them,
Thongs criss-cross to his knees,
With short Arcadian skirt,
A stripling, brown and roughened by the sun.
Limpid breezes,
Running slim fingers through his burnt black hair,
Have touselled it to elf-locks;
Slender and straight,
His thighs are hardened to the upward pull.
Companionless he goes, half insolent,
His crook behind his shoulders,
A smile behind his lips,
A tuft of golden crocus buds
In one cold hand.
His arrogant unamorous eyes, brook-brown,
Scorn to laugh, though flickering with laughter.
The pasture ground is reached,
A rocky hillside, rank with asphodel,
Beneath the temple ruin shepherds know—

ENZIO'S KINGDOM

Bassae, the healing god's gray windy house.
The flock apprize the field with yellow eyes,
Shallow and cold,
Then scatter, some
On hind legs reaching for the wet cool buds
Of stunted trees,
Some browsing where the scentless heliotrope
Patterns the ground with white and lilac bloom.
Below,
The brook sends up a breezy sound
From clustered laurel trees
That gad its mirrory lengths along
To watch the crimson fillets of their buds,
That smell and open to the passionate sun.
He stops, lays down his crook,
Then, catching up the world in one sure glance,
Draws from his leathern belt
The uncouth shepherd's flute,
Perches him on a ledge of seeded grasses
And, knees drawn up,
Fills it with steady breath.
His cheeks swell out;
His neck strains into chords,
Crimsons beneath the tan;
His mischievous eyes tilt upward in delight,
And raucous happy sounds insult the dawn.

Shadows whisk in the temple portico,
Advance on shaggy feet,
Drop down, again advance,
Scurry from bush to bush,
And crowd at last

AN ARCADIAN IDYLL

The crest of hills that half encircle him
Noisy below.
But he pipes on and only hears his piping,
And never sees for all his laughing glances
Flat in the dew, with chin on hand and ears pricked
 up,
Biting a wisp of feathered grass,
The little wood-gods
Listening.

A BRITTANY IDYLL

Far, far from here,
By Tristan's isle,
The bay awaits the breeze,
Paler than harebells breathed on by the dew,
Paler than turquoise, for the dawn is young
And single stars yet shine above Douarnenez. . . .
An easterly wind at sunset blew the fishing fleet
From its safe harborage beneath the town
Into the sunset.
With single sails they flew,
Yellow and brown and carmine-stained,
Across the blinding mirrors of the bay,
Beneath the tawny sunset flared with blue,
Beyond the western portals of the world.
But where the cold Atlantic waters, hoar and black,
Catch on their sleek enormous rhythms slurs of stars,
They lowered sail, and rocked upon the swell.
Then nets were cast and glimmering sank,
And night long, with few words
But mighty laborings,
The fisher-folk hauled in the flickering catch.
Beneath the stars they toiled, on ocean's floor.

But now the night is passing,
Leaving a silver wake
And aster petals halfway up the sky.
It is a lover's sunrise:
Lavender and gray and shining pink,

A BRITTANY IDYLL

A tilted sea-shell's inner opulence.
Beyond the jetty that the town throws out
For harborage and home to little boats,
The concave waves are dappled with rose leaves
And floats of foam.
At the jetty's end, far out from shore,
Nearest the point where turning in
From open water to calm anchorage
The fishing-fleet sails past,
A girl is standing.
And only she and the sunrise and wavering gulls
See the curves of rustling tide run in
And hear the calm world's breathing.
She is not lonely
For all her loneliness,
There in the summer sunrise,
With her simple peasant's dress of black,
Her meagre shawl of black crochet,
And her peasant's cap, looped and starched and white,
Prim on her pale gold hair.
Her arms are idly spread across the coping,
Her eyes turn always seaward, for she knows
Soon will the ships come home on the gales of morning,
Soon her lover's ship, and her tall brown lover,
The sailor-lad, soft-spoken, who is hers.
And he will smile to her his secret smile,
Tending the tiller as the boat swings past,
And wave to her as if to all he waved,
And meet her eyes with his, then look away.
Her lids are lowered and her lips just smile,
For she is conjuring in dream those eyes—
Bitter and bright and blue,

ENZIO'S KINGDOM

Like thin-topped waves against the sun,
The eyes men fear—
But she knows they can warm and seem to touch
Resistlessly.

And all the while she hums forgetfully
An old, old song the Breton girls have sung
Since first they loved and feared
And eased their hearts in song
(Perhaps Iseult of Brittany
Was humming the same words in that same place
A thousand years ago,
What time she waited for Lord Tristan
Whom she loved so grievously):

> *My only love is a sailor lad*
> *Whose home is the fickle sea.*
> *To other girls he gives his smiles,*
> *But his mouth he gives to me.*
>
> *On Sunday morning after mass*
> *When he is dressed so fine,*
> *He stops before their open doors,*
> *But at night he comes to mine.*
>
> *O Mary, bless all sailor lads*
> *Whose loves are two and three,*
> *But mine keep safe from other girls—*
> *Or let him die in the sea!*

And as the last line leaves her lips
She pauses, puckers up her mild girl's brow,
Then laughs a low contented laugh,
And sings again, half crooningly.

A BRITTANY IDYLL

But summer sunshine, jubilant with cock-crows,
Is rattling open all the shuttered town.
The cross-roads gild, and housewives with their mops
Splash on the family door-step; street by street
Hears emptily the melancholy calls,
Reiterant and shrill, of country women,
Shoving their push-carts full of salad leaves
And gasping fish and lentils, frosty green.
Soon shore and beach and jetty are swarming and laughing
With fishermen's wives and mothers
And fathers and children and friends,
Come down to welcome the fleet:
Old men with cautious, simple eyes
And polished wrinkles carved in wood,
Old women coiffed in white
With wide clean aprons, baskets on their arms,
And little boys with windy looks and sober ways,
Breeched and jumpered in mandarin sail-cloth—
All shuffling in wooden shoes
That clatter and thump on the cobbles—
And the girl at the end of the jetty
Among them and of them,
Laughing the laughter that hides.
At last the black line of the wind appears,
Dragging behind unevenly the fleet.
And instantly the shore is ruffled
With ant-hill runnings up and down,
And pointing hands and voluble, unheeded chatter.
But she is silent,
Clutching her shawl in the freshening breeze,

And pale—or pale as peasant girls may be—
For the fishing boats are returning
And the sailors return from the sea.
Moth after moth, gold-winged on the golden morning,
Bursting and drinking the light green spray of the tide,
They fly with flashing and splendor out of the ocean,
Straining for waters of calm and the haven they know.
As each ship rounds the mole with sail careening
The girl leans out,
Searching the weathered faces of the crew.
And now her lover's boat flings past,
Wrapped in a dazzle of spray, dripping with brine,
Tilting its saffron sail in the rainbow wash
As it shoulders the mole.
Ah, the girl is a pendent flower!
Her mouth, her eyes, her soul,
Above him, gazing, waiting!
But he, forgetful, wrangles with the ropes,
And never lifts his head, nor waves his hand,
Nor sends one smile
Up to her eager face.
And the last late boat comes home,
And the fishing's done,
And hulls are emptied of their freight—
Mauve and silver-scaled sardines—
And sails are furled
And in the quiet sunlight from the masts
The nets are hung to dry—
The sea-soaked azure nets,
Bluer than filaments of unflawed turquoise.

A BRITTANY IDYLL

But the girl alone on the bright deserted jetty
Still stands in the staring sunshine,
Her warm breast leaned against the spray-damp coping
It leaned more warmly on when he passed by.
But now her head is crouched behind her arms,
Her shawl clutched to her mouth,
And out across the hazing sea her wide eyes stare
Unseeingly and full of fear.

And the ancient wind from Tristan's isle comes sighing,
From the isle where long ago
Iseult with white hands folded on her lap,
Night after night,
Before the smouldering faggot fire,
Sat watching for some little tenderness
From Tristan,
Tristan the knight, whose heart to Cornwall clave
Unpityingly,
As all men know.

DELTA SKETCHES

IN THE DELTA

The river country's wide and flat
  And blurred ash-blue with sun,
And there all work is dreams come true,
  All dreams are work begun.

The silted river made for us
  The black and mellow soil
And taught us as we conquered him
  Courage and faith and toil.

The river town that water oaks
  And myrtles hide and bless
Has broken every law except
  The law of kindliness.

And north and south and east the fields
  Of cotton close it round,
Where golden billows of the sun
  Break with no shade or sound.

Dear is the town, but in the fields
  A little house could be,
If built with care and auspices,
  A heart's felicity.

O friend, who love not much indoors
  Or lamp-lit, peopled ways,
What of a field and house to pass
  Our residue of days?

ENZIO'S KINGDOM

We'd learn of fret and labor there
  A patience that we miss
And be content content to be
  Nor wish nor hope for bliss.

With the immense untrammelled sun
  For brother in the fields,
And every night the stars' crusade
  Flashing to us their shields,

We'd meet, perhaps, some dusk as we
  Turned home to well-earned rest,
Unhurried Wisdom, tender-eyed,
  A pilgrim and our guest.

GREENVILLE TREES

The Lombardy Poplars:

CAPTIVE in this drab alien land,
We dreamed of all the great and wise
Who took the roads our shadows spanned
With song on lips and sword on thighs.

King Richard fared, one morn of May,
Our leafy lane to Palestine
With Blondel following. Well-a-day,
They sang of God and love and wine!

We leaned to pity once that girl
Who left the Loire one dripping spring,
So red of mouth, so brown of curl,
To be love's slave and Scotland's king.

Crusaders, knights, and troubadours
Rode through our golden-panelled shade:
We never thought these songless shores
Could rival that dead cavalcade.

But, petulant of simple joys,
Loving Death's mother, blind Romance,
We watched the passionate Delta boys
Stride down the street that leads to France.

The China-Berries:

THOUSANDS of years ago,
We were weaving in moonlit Manchu gardens

Webs and arabesques of purple
On the moon-gray pebbled paths
For slender empresses,
In silver, lavender, and rose,
To tread on with their fuchsia-tinted sandals.
And one, on such a night,
Paused in our falling veils of subtle fragrance
And lifted up her arms
To the weary, much-prayed-to moon,
And wept for love.
But we have never seen these pale new people
Lift their arms to the exquisite moon
Or linger in our perfume.
They seem unconscious
Of the marvel of our blossoms,
Our stamens purpler-black than clematis,
Our delicate wisteria-tinged corolla.
Yet slender-fingered undulant princesses
Have bit their coral lips
And slain in anger
Prostrate imperial attendants
Because no loom could match our secret dyes.

Here we must tolerate small girls
With strange, sun-colored hair
Who thread our blossoms
And loop them with coarse clover-chains
About their throats.
Or worse, near summer-time,
Small boys, with eyes that have no darkness,
Will clamber into our branches,
Wounding our tender bark of satin,

GREENVILLE TREES

Snapping our wonderful patterned leaves,
And pull our berries,
Hard, green, with infinitesimal speckles;
Then filling our indignant shade with laughter,
Jolly, uncouth, immoderate,
Mash them into their popguns
And frighten the sparrows even
And the reverent ancient negroes
With their insolent bombardment. . . .

Only the winter robins love us,
And then our boughs are naked,
And our shrivelled berries
Hang down in milky yellow clusters,
Fingered by faded winds,
Against a gray interminable sky.
Yet then too we are beautiful!

The Locusts:

In vain we fill the winter's palms
With rush of round, thin, golden alms.
The winter has no care for us
But breaks our brittle branches thus,
    Abjuring calms.

Yet one week of the year is ours:
We sun our creamy, scented flowers
And madden all the town. Oh, they
Are powerless, though prim, to stay
    Our fragrant powers.

ENZIO'S KINGDOM

The crowded church we bloom before
Leaves carelessly an open door:
Young sinners' eyes desert their books
And meet with long-lashed pagan looks
    And read no more.

Ah, watch for them, when shadows wait,
Walking the levee, slow, sedate!
But blush to guess the darling sights
When perfumes are the only lights,
    And it grows late.

The Water Oaks:

ONCE in our branches
Swarms of green parrakeets in seething turmoil settled,
Chattering north from the sweltering rank pampas,
Clothing us doubly in delightful leaves,
And suddenly departing.
But long ago, one violet spring,
We watched their wavering throngs melt down the south
To come again no more. . . .
We have been darkened by clouds of pigeons
Weltering like a cyclone
Across the watery rose sunset.
But some great death
Slew them: they come no more. . . .
More beautiful than all the wings that fly in beauty,
The wild swans,
Noble and full of fellowship,

GREENVILLE TREES

Came in old days
Down the broad curves and brimming tremble of the river,
Or overland, at night, against the stars.
Oppressed with solemn joy
And ever-urgent purpose undisclosed,
They hovered in the twilight of cool autumn
Or mounted on the sunrise, trumpeting
And glad of rest, though brief.
For all their beauty
Each year we saw their glistening ranks dissolve,
Dissolve and waste, till now
Once in a winter and with pain
We spy perhaps a lone white wanderer,
Mateless and without friend,
Circling uncertainly and with hoarse piteous cries,
Till mercifully, with no thought of mercy,
The gray-eyed hunter on the river bars,
Making of murder sport, deprives
Him of his loneliness, the deep sky of a swan.
So too the races passed that lived beneath our leaves—
The patient, thought-pressed builders of the mounds
That came from mystery,
Returning whence they came;
The stealthy copper tribes
Whose arrows slit the blue beyond our heights,
Who, making moonlight haggard with their fires,
Danced in bad triumph at their brothers' death,
But in the end found never a cause to dance.
So too shall pass their pallid conquerors
Who now in slaying us have made the land
Naked and without loveliness of shade.

Though they have planted seed where once we towered
And hemmed the river's strength
And wedged us in their curveless hot-floored towns,
They too shall pass,
And we shall watch them die.

In the beginning there were three
And in the end there shall be only three:
The trees, the river,
And the outspread lonely tree of heaven,
Whose boughs are blossomy apple-wreaths at dawn,
Autumnal red and purple in the sunset,
And laden, night long, with the fruitage of the stars,
A harvest for some still-delaying husbandman.

THE HOLY WOMEN

I have seen Mary at the cross
    And Mary at the tomb
And Mary weeping as she spread her hair
    In a leper's room.

But it was not in Bethany
    Or groping up Calvary hill
I learned how women break their hearts to ease
    Another's ill.

Compassionate and wise in pain,
    Most faithful in defeat,
The holy Marys I have watched and loved
    Live on our street.

A BURNISHED CALM

If I could be as calm as willow branches
When the sunlight turns them copper-pink and gold
And they lift their slender wands in the winter sunshine
From out the red-brown coffee-weeds into the blueness;
If I could know the calm of willow branches
When the hollows of the woods hold azure smoke
And the southern winter blurs and tarnishes;
If I could feel their passive unstrained certainty
As they wait the still-uneager, leaf-laden springtime,
Not fearing it will never come or come
Less beautiful, not doubting the return in time
Of downy buds and wrinkled burgeoning
And all the filmy lustre of warm days;
If I could be like willows by the river-bank in winter,
I think that wars remembered and presaged,
The drugging sense of doom and old disaster,
Would not oppress and strangle me as now.
But I should have a faith unflawed by these,
Discerning through the mad inclement now
The right's august recurrence in the race,
And like the leafless willows by the river
Wait in the winter sunshine trustfully
And with a burnished calm.

LEVEE NOCTURNE

A swan hangs brooding where the light
    Is colorless and cool—
Or is it but the moon above
    Her amethystine pool?

The powdered dusk is sifting down,
    The purple willows blur,
The air awaits its stars and bats
    And unseen moths that whir.

The houses light their lamps of gold
    Where bread is blessed and broken;
The noises of the day seem but
    A foolish word once spoken.

Only the quietness remains,
    So tender and so deep,
When the weary, weary pent-in-life
    Escape awhile in sleep.

A MEMORY

I saw four days of spring come floating down
Among the hard-gray lonely days of winter.
They came with full-blown warmth down the blue air
Like four pink petals shook from a loose wild rose
Or four pink clouds crossing an April sunrise
Or four young pilgrims stoled in misty rose,
Smelling of musk and with an Eastern grace.
And as they fell, softly, one after one,
On the shrivelled earth, delight returned, long absent:
The single trees in the fields, the many trees
In the woods, wrapped them in webs of rainbow gauze;
Lads dreamed of braided tresses, and the breeze
Of clear, clear water falling in pure sunlight;
Violets came, the purple and the gray
Wild sort that flaunt themselves and have no smell;
The jonquils trooped out in their sky-gold dresses,
Nodding and whispering like girls from school;
The great oaks seemed a haze the breeze might scatter,
Though blackbirds creaked and coughed on every
    bough;
The weeping willows, amber gales at anchor,
Danced in the rhythm of spring waterfalls;
And there was wistfulness and joy four days and
    nights.
Then came the frost:
The wizened buds lay speckled on the ground,
Winter came back, more bitter for its going.
Four days of spring and of a spring long past!

A MEMORY

You ask me why I should remember them?
If you had ever loved and been beloved,
Even so briefly as four days and nights,
You would remember many things perhaps
That now I think you do not even see.

SONG

Sorrowful leaves of the winter oak
That cannot fall and cannot flutter,
Clutching, with love too deep to utter,
The branches that loved you when green was your cloak—
Fall, fall, for your green is gone,
And none loves love for itself alone,
And a faithful lover's a worrisome thing
In the spring, the spring, the tender spring.

OUTCAST

A summer's twilight ramble brought me where
I too shall sleep, if prayers are answered still.
No sad particular errand led me there,
But thoughts I let, that evening, have their will.

The graves are very quiet in that light,
Simple, despite their angels and their urns;
"Asleep in Jesus," "Rest in Peace," the trite
Poor epitaphs, seem then the due one earns.

Each bore its name and date, and so appealed
To cherish what already was forgot;
Some still could boast of wreaths, some, hardly healed,
Of wilted flowers and a mown grass-plot.

I passed with half a smile and half a sigh,
And came to those wild grasses where they too,
With no rememberer to tend them, lie
With equal peace in hammocked rags of dew.

I found there, by a purple iron-weed
Hung with black beetles, one lone slab that bore
No name, no date, but only this strange screed:
"Nature, who played the trick, can laugh no more."

Whether that outcast grave was tenanted
Or waits for one still walking earth's wide floor
I knew not, yet in fear I stooped and read:
"Nature, who played the trick, can laugh no more."

THE DELTA AUTUMN

Give me an ebbing sunset of the fall
With chilly flare of cosmos-colored light,
A white-winged moon in frozen, downward flight,
Ethereal, naked trees where no birds call;
Leave me to watch my infinite, gaunt river,
Its solemn width, its willow-purpled coil,
Its floor of hammered brass and azure oil,
Its silence where far strands of wild geese quiver—
And I'll not miss the hopeful, passionate spring,
Spring that knows naught of thought or masterful will
Or conquered grief or peace when cold winds chill,
But sings and struts with sunlight-dabbled wing
And is too sweet where men yet hate and kill.
Autumn as autumn comes in my dim-lustered land—
Of that be my dreaming under the fennel-crusted sand.

A LETTER FROM JOHN KEATS
TO FANNY BRAWNE

A LETTER FROM JOHN KEATS TO FANNY BRAWNE

Rome, December, 1820.

I HAD not thought to ever taste again
The mellowness of living. But today
The fever's less, the creeping end is only
A warm tide of luxurious weariness
And steady, rich discernment, rare of late.
This mild Italian autumn of tarnished leaves,
The sunshine thick like yellow muscadel
With nectarous smell of overripe bruised fruits,
The autumn feel of pause, accomplishment,
Finality almost, and tears behind,
Have so infected me with their serene
That I experience wisdom without wisdom's pain. . . .
I can recall such hours before we met,
But none or few thereafter. . . . No, that's not true:
No wisdom calmed my days before we met;
Their best was heartless crystalline delight,
Such as a bird must feel mounting the sunrise;
While this mood in its peace seems posthumous,
The spent year's spell, in which I see my life
And all our love rounded and closed like music. . . .
Now in a day or two, at most a month,
I shall be sleeping in a dreamy place
Where Severn says the springtime is wet blue
With violets and smoothest red and white
With cool camellias, fit for tapestry.

ENZIO'S KINGDOM

You must not worry. 'Twill be a quiet sleeping
Under this sky, so beautiful, yet not
The sky of home. . . . Before that dull time comes
I must unvenom all my old reproaches
And tell you how, gauging the whole strange tale
Of our sweet love, I find there only comfort—
No anguish, no regret—and in my heart
Nothing of love except love's tenderness.

I thought, I tried to think, my suffering
Was passion's unfulfilment, the divorce
Of you and me by poverty, disease.
But now I know—I always knew, I think—
The cause was simpler and incurable.
That I have suffered from this love of ours
You know too well for me in kindness now
To half gainsay. But you could never know
How much your hand at rest on Brown's firm shoulder
Above my invalid's chair could torture me;
Or how, when your so longed-for letters came—
That never said enough—I had no strength
To open them, but covered them with kisses,
Like any scullery maid, and broke the seal
Each time with all the dreadful pang of heartbreak.
Ah, pain enough, dear girl, and pain to spare,
But through no fault of yours, for you are faultless!
At last I dare to recognize the cause
Of why I found love like a bloody sweat:
You could not love me but in your own way,
And that—that was a way that was not mine.
I had known much of grief, too much of death,
And never been the comrade of good fortune;

A LETTER FROM JOHN KEATS TO FANNY BRAWNE

My passion had no lightness and no grace,
It burned me up—a death pyre by the sea
At night, its red light putting out the stars.
There was no moment of the day or night
I did not hunger for you. I saw your face,
Your throat, your hair, more real, more tangible
Than anything within my true eyes' vision;
Your rare low words of love, your thoughtless laughter,
Haunted my hearing like a song remembered. . . .
I cannot think what my love meeting love
As fearful as itself had ended in!
Yours was the love it met, and so that thought
Is speculative. . . . Yours was the love, my dearest,
And you were just eighteen—not Guinevere,
Francesca, or Iseult, but merely Fanny—
If less than they in majesty of mind,
Their equal in the accident of beauty.
How could I hope that I could be to you
The rudiment and base of happiness,
The dovecote of all thoughts, the fold of dreams,
The desert fountain, as you were to me?
Who had expected, if the fragrant Psyche
Had fled from Greece and turned an English girl,
That she should mourn all day the missing Eros
And not be friendly with the English boys,
Touching their hands and dancing in their dances,
Laughing with them, untroubled by her love?
It was too much to hope that you should sicken
Because love wounded me. You loved me—yes—
And were as kind as mothers to their children.
But, oh, you loved me with a girl's light love,

And could have loved as easily another!
That was the unslaked thirsting of my life
And that the poisoned knowledge I abhorred. . . .
You see how gentleness was difficult
And why ofttimes I blamed you without cause,
Conceding not at all that you and I
Were made to hurt each other, being made
By different gods, in different moods, removed
By nature and conjoined by cynic chance.

That's past; forget with me its bitterness,
Remembering instead that out of this
Impossible, precipitous, starved love
Came all that I may claim of worth and beauty—
(I'd like to think you'd care to read these words
Slowly and more than once, they mean so much)—
You, who took all I had, gave all I have.
You were not wholly Madeleine, perhaps,
Nor even that Belle Dame who wrought such woe,
But had your loveliness not pierced my soul
And stolen my peace and made me friend of anguish,
I should have written in their stead, no doubt,
Another and as poor Endymion.
Even the nightingale was poignant by
Your absence, and lacking you I learned of her
Her secret, and found me shelter from love's cold
In beauty's house. . . . My glistening perfect garlands,
Woven of ilex dark and polished bay,
Should not in justice lie across the threshold
Of that high temple of the god of song,
But on your doorstep, like a sweetheart's posy.

A LETTER FROM JOHN KEATS TO FANNY BRAWNE

Then, too, love brings with his fine cruelty
Such fellowship of tears and sense of sorrow!
Without you I was intimate with gods
And sylvan deities and fairy folk,
Wept at romances in a dog-eared book,
And found a song more moving than live pain.
But these last days, with all my singing stopped,
I am amazed to find stored up in me
Compassion's very substance and a glow
Of human pity never dreamed before.
I see my kinship with the dreadful world
And, healed of youthful blindness, recognize
The brotherhood of grief. There is no warmth
Of poesy or bliss so purged and fierce
As this that laves about my naked heart
Since I have made discovery of man.
I watch them from my window here at Rome,
And not a face but tells beneath its masque
Of some such commonplace as death or fear
Or passion starved or passion fed to grossness.
And in the night when Severn thinks I sleep
I watch the pale processional stream past—
Humanity, like wounded from a battle.
Oh, all the eyes quenched out that once were stars!
Oh, all the lips that sag and blench with pain!
Eternal loneliness in search of love!
I know their secret, taste their hidden tears,
And, one of them, to each one stretch my arms. . . .
Aged twenty-four! And as I'm leaving it
I understand the world—because of you!
Shakespeare, you know, had fifty years or more,
Yet I could talk with him and not feel young.

ENZIO'S KINGDOM

Well, I'll not keep you longer reading words
That may or may not have a meaning in them.
Severn (who should be friendship's synonym
And lacks in nothing but a woman's touch)
Will soon be running up the stairs and stand
Aghast to find me wasting thus my strength.
When I have calmed him I shall beg for those
Light-hearted and ethereal filigrees
Haydn and Mozart made of silver sound.
They cool me . . . almost as much as one cool hand
That used to stroke my forehead. Oh, not yet,
Not yet, ask me to write the last farewell!
I wish it could be just one breathed caress,
Lingering, like a prayer, and unlike those
You were familiar with and maybe loved.
O Fanny, how I long for you to fathom
All, all the tenderness and thanks I feel,
Here turning in the doorway of dumb death,
For you. You are so far away and lonely!
I see you as the wistfulest thing alive,
So young and unadvised and full of joy,
Irrevocably travelling down the years
To meet irrevocable dark misfortune,
With beauty for your weak and sole defense
And lust of living for your only guide.
Not to be close where you could call to me,
Not to lean over you when tears must come
And you be trampled by the brutal world—
There's the one last regret that dying has! . . .
Someone will take my place in that respect. . . .
I will not say I envy him—O God—

A LETTER FROM JOHN KEATS TO FANNY BRAWNE

But that I wish him some such gentleness
As mine, and power to protect far greater. . . .
Do not remember me if memory hurts.
Good-bye, bright star, good-bye. God bless you, Fanny.

ENZIO'S KINGDOM

ENZIO'S KINGDOM

Dead, then, the most imperial of emperors
And by some accident of flesh my father!
I am content, Berard; nay, I am glad.
Life's infamy was overgalling to him.
He suffered like a god that had no part
In its creation, but was resolved—how madly—
To make it over, if not beautiful,
Tolerable at least and roomed for men.
And then, Berard, his godlike loneliness
With only you and me to lean upon!
I but a gold-haired bastard lad and you
An old man sworn to serve the Church he loathed,
Forsworn for love of him; and both of us
Brimmed and surbrimmed by his enormous dreams
And alchemized in his fond fiery love—
But of ourselves unmeriting and common.
How could all nature not rise up and be
His partisan? How could he fail, Berard,
Unless the very dastard race of men
He suffered for deserve its doom of failure?

But I forget the laws of courtesy,
Remembered first, and last forgot by him.
The night is late and you have travelled far
And secretly to tell me of his death.
I should say words of thanks and let you go.
Your hand shakes and you have great need of sleep—
We both have need of sleep, I think—long sleep.

ENZIO'S KINGDOM

But O, Berard, when that door clangs behind you
It will not ever open on a friend;
And I, the young king of Sardinia,
The emperor's son, will be a tame pet prisoner
Till the end, till the long sleep we need so.
Sit down, I pray you: let me talk of him—
Of him they call the Second Frederick,
But I call father. Tears—ah! And in your eyes.
How many times I've wept so at your knee!

You knew him from his birth, as you knew me,
For which I have it in my heart to envy you.
I've often wondered of that little boy
With red wild hair and sultry shadowed eyes,
Orphaned and penniless, the old Pope's ward,
An unwished, scanted guest from house to house
Among the ignorant burghers of Palermo—
Despite which the incorrigible heir
Of Barbarossa's and blond Guiscard's blood.
Those years of vile neglect and unjust anguish
Were often in his eyes, when fixed on me,
And made, I think, the passionate tenderness
Of his solicitude and vigilant love.
I was to be all he had never been—
The darling citizen of his new world;
Delight's own bosom friend; above all, free.
Now he is dead, his rosy world salt red,
And I the citizen of four wet walls,
Of freedom and of father both bereft!
If he had been content to merely be
The Kingdom's king, the lord of Sicily:
If when great Barbarossa's heavy crown

ENZIO'S KINGDOM

Was tendered to his brows uncrowned with manhood
He had refused it, had not dashed with you
And that gay handful of adventurers
To Constance, crashed the gates to, laughed at Otho—
Today he might be hawking in the Kingdom,
Or matching rhymes with young-voiced troubadours,
Or naming stars with some lean Arab seer:
And I'd be hearing still his great clean laugh.
But then he had been an oblivion's king,
Not Frederick, the Wonder of the World,
The Torch shook out one great amazed short instant,
Then dashed, to leave for us intenser dark. . . .

Within this nothingness ahead, I'll try
Forgetting of the smoky latter years,
The blood spilled and the failure, and solace me
With dreaming of his dream when it was true—
At least it seemed so once in our Palermo.
'Tis not the rich deceptive blue of retrospect
Makes so serenely excellent those days
When you and I, Pietro and Thaddeus,
Were cornerstones of his imperial life,
Miraculously graven with his love.
There never was on earth such dowered peace,
Such laughter blowing through old wisdom's cell,
Such intellect shot like a proud gold arrow
Into the giant freedom of the sun!
Mere memory of those times is more alive
Than the brash breathing days allowed most mortals!
That room, Berard, that opened on the sea,
Full of slant sunbeams in the afternoon,
Where he revised the idiot world's affairs

ENZIO'S KINGDOM

With you by as grave councillor and me,
No taller than a broadsword, listening,
Quite gravely too, as like as not my head
Against his knee, beneath his hovering hand—
That room touched with its inmate light the lengths
Of Araby, Illyria, England, Greece,
Dazzled outlandish folk beyond the Rhine,
Warmed Aragon, Provence, dull Austria,
And flared our own obscure sweet Sicily
Into the day-star of a starless night.
I'd listen in a blinking glow of wonder
To orders, laws, decisions, policies:
A fleet to Reggio; a thousand men to Jaffa;
A brace of falcons to the king of France;
To our belovèd vassals of Cologne
A charter and the right of toll; requests
For cotton and the barley seed he promised
Of Sultan Kamel, our especial friend,
Appended to a note on Aristotle;
Exemption of all silk looms from taxation;
Death for a judge whose greed was not for justice;
Appointment of a notary for Flanders,
A seneschal for Treves, a captain for
The ships of oil and wheat outbound for India;
Our thanks to Brother Leo for the copy
Of that last Canticle as Francis wrote it,
Enclosing our own manuscript on hawking;
An edict granting freedom to the Jews:
The whole a brave clear text of liberal wisdom
Illumined with light-hearted blue and gold!
The pageant of the world passed through that room,
Their colors burning in the moted sunlight—

ENZIO'S KINGDOM

Ambassadors and pilgrims, knights and seers,
Star-gazers, troubadours, philosophers,
The wise, the wisdom-seeking, the renowned.
The race's best and foremost swarmed to him
As night-things to a streaming far-seen light.

But when the day was over, the candles lit,
The last petitioner gone, the empire's needs
Dismissed till morning, then it was, Berard,
The day began, for then we were alone.
He'd think aloud to me, pacing the room's length
Or standing mute, one hand lost in his beard,
His brain the battle-ground of two strong thoughts.
'Twas then the infinite details of his task
Assembled in perspective, and resolved
To fractions of his intricate patterned dream.
And when his vehement revery was done
That smile he had for me would quite uncloud
His face, and with one arm about my shoulder
He'd pass out to the sea-cooled balcony
Where the full darkness fell and no sound stole.
And he would stand there silent a long while,
Watching in a profound remote repose
The multitudinous slow flight of stars,
All hush and ecstasy, or, far beneath,
The bleak silver ocean barred with black,
Calm as eternity, though quivering always.
Then he would say: "Now let us sleep, my son.
The infinitudes of beauty with no toil
Pursue their ministries we may not guess,
Though vibrant to the music they exhale:
Our waking or our sleep will vex them not."

He was aware no keenlier of the actual
Than of the instigating powers that buoy us.
Caesar, I think, nor Alexander saw
So rightly nor so far into the dark.

The day that thrust me suddenly from boy's
To man's estate shines yet through fifteen years.
It was the day he honored Michael Scott
As though the king of India were his guest,
Not some pinched nobody in broidered gown
Of stars and moons and suns and hieroglyphs,
Who dubbed himself astrologer and watched
Dancing girls, rabbis, princes, desert sheiks—
The palace-full assembled in his honor—
In the cold English way and never laughed.
But most, I found, he watched my glowing father,
Single in debonair and gracious ease
Among the guests. And I could swear, Berard,
There was some dry and cynic pity in his gaze.
Then Pietro asked him, in a voice all heard,
What was the emperor's own fated star.
With his thin smile and pale satiric eyes
He answered in a blight of sudden silence
"Canopus," and again the silence closed.
My father's laugh was shorter than his words:
"A star so small his very name's unknown."
"Ask of your Arab friends," the wizard's voice
Ran smooth as ice: "In fiery magnitude
He is the greatest of all stars." "Then why,"
Pursued my father, "should I have never seen
His flaming orb?" There was a long strange pause.
At last the answer came, but hardly heard:

"He is too bright for our cold northern skies.
They see him but an instant, then he goes."
My father laughed, "Thanks for a brilliant moment,"
And with accustomed calm and showered banter
Passed through the company. Alone with me,
In silence that seemed almost sorrowful,
He reached the room I loved and sat awhile
In some abstracted lassitude of thought,
While I, boylike, wished Michael Scott were dead.
Thus da Vigna found us.

                O even now
'Tis hard to hate da Vigna—and then he seemed
The perfect knight; as poet, councillor,
Vice-regent, friend, the nonpareil and pattern.
There was such glitter of resolve about him,
Such frankness, yet such reticence of mood,
As if he were a quarrying hawk that hovered
For game far off before he flashed and struck.
Ah, well, that night he only came to reckon
What stallions would be needed for Apulia,
And how Phoenician trade might be drawn off
From Genoa and the purple ships of Venice.
Pietro da Vigna leaned across the table
Fingering maps and schedules while my father,
Sunk in his cushioned chair almost a throne,
Listened, the weavings of his burnished gown
Seeming to breathe in the gold-spun candlelight.
Then Pietro said the rebel town of Bari—
To capture which was his express stout task—
Had not yet fallen, nay, it would not fall
Until a further complement of men

Was furnished them that had attacked in vain.
There was a panther stir in the great chair.
"I have no men to send you," came his voice.
"Then Bari holds out till the crack o' doom,"
Broke bitterly from Pietro. My father grew
Stone still, and when his voice at last whipped out
It was no friendly voice: "Why ask for men
Before you have exhausted gold and guile?"
Da Vigna's hand went dead among his papers
And dead his face, except his eyes that winced.
But he was silent. Again the emperor spoke:
"Bribe them: or feast their leaders at a truce
And poison them." Pietro at that leaped up,
Pale truly, but a thousand miles from fear:
"Bribe or assassinate, your Majesty,
But find a fitter tool for such base work."
His voice was steady challenge and despair.
I shut my eyes so that I might not see
My father's terrible anger boiling up,
But when I looked his chin was on his hand
And he regarded Pietro dreamily
And from a cold great distance. Then he said,
As if in weariness: "Sit down: compose
That answer to the Pope we planned together,
While I have Enzio read aloud to me
His last translation from the happy Greek.
His Arab master found it in Byzantium."
So, gulping down the terror I had felt,
I found the manuscript, leaned back against
His knees, and while da Vigna seemed to write
And he to sleep, for he was breathless-still,

With eyelids closed, I read aloud to him.
And the very candles seemed to fall asleep.

It was the story of the son of Helios,
His gold-haired only son, not yet a man,
Who, watching his divinely sinewed father
Drive from the stables of the dark each dawn
The chariot and horses of the sun,
Besought that he might be their driver once
And for one glorying lonely day race up
The azure mountain of the infinite air.
And dotingly his father gave him leave,
While his young sisters of the clear gold hair
Wept for him as they wandered by the river
Gathering hyacinths. But who may bear
The burden of all light through solitude
Except a god? Or, swathed in dizzy foam
Of hissing manes, hold to their difficult course
Those passionate stallions fed on naked fire?
Half up the sky, seething in whirlwind light,
He gazed in anguish on the earth he knew,
The friendly, populous earth, dappled with shade,
And through his sweat-bright hands the taut reins slipped.
Down plunged the horses, down the chariot plunged;
And like a meteor in full day descried
Headlong the gold-haired son of Helios fell—
Silent and lovely, his hand before his eyes. . . .
I ceased. There was great quietness, except
My father's hand was groping in my hair.
It seemed he had been speaking ere he spoke:
"But thou shalt never fall, my son, nor guide

ENZIO'S KINGDOM

Alone the golden chariot of the sun.
My hands shall grasp the reins and close beside me
Thou shalt behold the turmoil of my sky,
The sweetness of thine earth, smiling, untroubled.''

He rose and paced the floor his pauseful way
When brooding, and smouldered as he dreamed aloud:
"For mankind in the mass, truth is what works—
A creed, a fair illusion, a reward;—
Some worthy lie by which they shuffle through
In something that approaches happiness.
Not their content nor their accomplishment
Are for the few whose greed is truth itself.
Our desolate and ice-cold consolation
Is that no matter what the vacancy
Unstarred and horrible we stumble on
In the scheme of things, it cannot be as bleak
And choking and insufferable as this
All-drowning ignorance we welter in.
For us there are no terrors and few joys,
But only courage and a blown bright hope . . .
To grip the tatterdemalion unsorted world
And make a plan of it—that's our occupation:
Preëminently mine, who in the chaos
Am thrust as ruler, and recognize indeed
My own mind as a mountain among hills.
Were I an indolent dreamer I could weep
At all the tongues and all the arrogant creeds
Disharmonizing man, obscuring his
Essential unity and native likeness,
And wish in futile wrath to blot them out.
Instead, not futilely, I grapple facts;

And spite of races, tongues and creeds at odds
Impose the unity of my bold justice
Upon a turbulent world from Nazareth
To Ghent. . . . That is the ground-work of all
   peace. . . .
Peace. Peace. The great prerequisite,
The race's single chance to reach its stature . . .
There's not a lie too great, a crime too gross
I'll not be guilty of, if so thereby
I may establish it and fix the lines
Of the quivering vision I intend the world. . . .
Am I the first that with sheer intellect
Has hated war, not weeping at its woe
So much as raging at its waste and folly?
Let me be first: and by the stablishment
Of peace I'll show my elders' errancy. . . .
And after peace I shall enchant the world
Into a universal Sicily
And prove life even can be livable. . . .

"Protect the masses in their breeding moil;
Feed them; and sweeten them by fear's remove:
But do not build for them, for they are doomed
To everyday contents and grievances—
Unspeculative, level, themselves their study.
But, oh, the flashing-eyed minority,
The Enzios of the world, the sons of light—
These I would turn free-pinioned on an earth
That they would make august and radiant!
Think, think, O gods, what freedom could mean here,
Freedom to think and be and to pursue
The sovereign hope a stormy heart may spring!

ENZIO'S KINGDOM

Never have they been loosened from the toils
Of fear, and sin imagined, and old thoughts,
And ever at their elbows threatened priest
Or king or skeleton of fleshly want.
I'll change all this: and for imperial boon
Grant freedom to the spirits of the free.
Watch them: already they are homing to me,
And there's no man today not sworn my vassal
If Truth or High Endeavor be his liege.
So much to learn, forgot or never learned!
Such flight-room for the gold bird of the mind!
Such loveliness to build or paint or set
In colored words of leisure on a parchment!
Oh, I conceive a breathing-space, for men
Of vestured soul, grander than heaven; yea,
And possible, a point oft overlooked
In heavenly and terrestial dreams, I judge.
And what to hinder, save the allotted span
Some yokel with a home-made stave may skimp?
So far I've won: my laws establish justice,
Justice peace, and the young future teems
To Naples and Salerno where my schools
Are aids and urgers to the starrier way.
My present is a sunny sky: but clouds
Unquietly from two bad quarters stir
And grope to make one storm, a storm so vast
It will blind out the opulent, life-giving sun. . . .
The rabble Lombard cities; and the Pope . . .
Can these bring back the ancient dark despite me?
Never. Never. Yet they draw off my force,
Like unjust judges; traitors; rebel cities—
Details a friend could spare me by assuming—

And I must close with them in battle. First,
The cities—orgulous, pestilently brave,
The pack of them fanging and foaming each on each
Like rutting dogs, and with the minds, means,
Manners of dogs. At large they bait the world
To brawls and bickerings, costly and futile:
But chained are frenzied martyrs howling 'Freedom,'
A word they fight for, but a fact, God knows,
They neither put to use nor grant to others.
The cities first: blood wasted and much gold,
But victory, the atrocious north restrained
And muzzled into manners and address. . . .
Then, Rome. . . . A struggle to the death, I fear. . . .
The war 'twixt emperors and popes will reach
In me its apogee, for good or ill.
Not that inherent differences appear
In Gregory's gage flung down to Frederick
And Hildebrand's to Barbarossa, but
The princes of the church divine in me
A serpent wiser and more venomous
Than in my crusty and impetuous grandsire.
He had perspective and fine taste for power
But was in fact a simple, loyal Christian.
While I—I see the thing that calls itself
Christ's Church a noble detriment, a dream
Once valid, but in the dawning old and evil.
I will concede the masses to the Pope:
Their stultified obedience makes for peace.
But I'll not give my eaglets to his cage:
For them there shall be freedom if it takes
The very toppling down of Peter's throne. . . .

"How blistered is the earth with outpoured blood
Which on the ground has but a human look—
Not Christian, Jewish, or Mohammedan!
They slaughter each the other in the name
Of Allah, Christ, Jehovah, that one god
Who needs a name to be distinguishable.
And now in Albi they would further tear
Their Christian sect of Rome into another,
And later still another, and another,
Till down the centuries the jargon of
Their creeds will rile, I swear, sweet-tempered Heaven!
Three is enough! I join with Rome at Albi
To drown this heresy in good French blood.
Three is enough: yet not enough, I know. . . .
Jesus, Mahomet, Abraham—good men
Guessing! I read their words with reverence
And know that still the ultimate word's not
    written. . . .
When I have made my tablet of the laws
To guide the flight of my young Enzios,
'Thou shalt not' shall be missing from its rubric.
Perhaps two words will make its decalogue:
'Courage: Unselfishness.' These two suffice.
Oh, all this cry of 'sin,' these acts forbidden,
Ruffle my gorge! The Christian sins if meat
Is eat on Friday; the Jew if any day
He eats of pork; the Prophet's follower
If anything on any day he eats
With Jew or Christian at his friendly table.
Fools, fools, and serious fools who die
For imbecilities diverse but equal!
With hortatives and childish talk of sin

They so have staled the cleanly natural air
That life stinks like a sick-room. Bah! their 'sin'—
There is no taint save its own consequence
To any deed; and what is wise is good!
The centuries' experience of a deed's
Outcome and burthen aids our judgment of it
Before 'tis done, but is not sacrosanct
Or final. If men would but forget what not
To do, and fix their wills and uttermost minds
On what to do and do it—they'd breed the world
With loveliness and power beyond all guessing!
Virtue is energy directed wisely:
And sin is sloth. . . . How am I judged here, now,
By this religious and oppressive world?
All I have wrought for justice and for peace,
For beauty's burgeoning and joy's flower,
Are these emblazoned on a scroll of praise?
Hardly. But I am damned as heretic,
And worse—an irony for Kamel—lecher!
I am not chaste, and so I spoil for hell!
These priests that never do the deed, but dream of it
Till their minds are porous—foetid—maggot's meat—
They grieve for me, who feed the monster I
Am caged in decently, I hope, and keep
My mind robust and cold as mountain wind. . . .
They do not even see the pity of it. . . .
How mockingly are our sweet bodies made
In that the very pang and leap of love
Is circumstanced in filth and sorry loathing!
And how wit-cursed the incarnating force
That fashions the idiot with no more pain
And no less air of nature justified

Than when a stripling god like Enzio's born!
No empress was your mother, Enzio;
But you were not begot half-heartedly,
Betwixt a dream and a sleep, the sanctioned way.

"But these are incidentals of a life
I purpose to make frank and vigorous. . . .
'Courage, Unselfishness,' and the youth of the world
At my heels! One could not fail with these nor shrink.
Truth sleeps and has indeed its evil dreams,
But never dies. . . . The Lombard cities scotched
And Rome's pretensions clipped, defined, made harmless,
I'll set the world upon a singing path
And rank it king-star of the heavenly host!
Such wisdom waits to be uncovered, Enzio,
Such loveliness to be evoked! O gods,
The splendor, majesty, and joy of life
Have not been tapped, but only wait upon
The spirit's franchise that I burn to grant. . . .
The chariot of the sun has issued forth,
The reins are in my hands—no turning back,
No stumbling, Enzio, nor halt, until
The azure circuit's run and regally
We rest our steeds in that mysterions stall—
Death's purple-raftered house. . . . Yet men stand back—
Men that should know and love me—baulk at some item,
Some Bari thrust between me and my purpose,
Which is today in the great staggering world
The only godlike, all-inclusive scheme
Of hope and betterment. . . . Was Helios lonely?"

He ceased, as if a great bell's toning ceased,
Leaving a chaos of grand sound and trembling.
Before the din had died, Pietro was speaking,
As tall and quiet-burning as a candle:
"Imperial master, grant me leave to go."
"Whither?" my father answered out of dimness.
"To Bari, which shall fall before this moon
Has shed her horns." Oh, it was good to hear
The wind of my father's laughter lift the shadows:
"Petrus, wound me no more so bitterly!
When we have built the new Jerusalem
Your name shall indicate right well your rank."
And from that day I was a boy no longer,
But saw his need of me and took my place.

That was the time life should have ceased, Berard,
Still fresh and glistening and mountain-aired,
Its only apprehension change or ending!
It is so grievous living past the prime
And looking back for all one's glimpse of glamour.
Surely no god who ever had been young
Could have watched idly so much loveliness
Undone! A wise and passionate innocence
Spangled our lives and made each hour awake
Keep the cool filmy fragrance of first waking. . . .
That passed too quickly—quicklier being lovely.
Our south, the south he loved so, saw him in
Pale lightning glimpses only after that night.
The storm was sooner breaking than he'd thought,
And never ended. Rome and the Lombard cities
Loosened their hate your news alone could quell.
Berard, Berard, it seems we have been fighting

ENZIO'S KINGDOM

Since the beginning of things, and all the rest's
A plaguing dream! And why it was—or when—
Or why it could not cease and let us be—
I cannot now remember. . . . Thanks, old friend. . . .
A faintness—yes—it's gone—the memories came
Too thick. . . . No, no, you cannot leave me yet!
Sleep is more torturing than weariness!
Just then when my eyes closed I saw his eyes—
Smoky with pain and void of recognition!
They make sleep full of fear: I cannot meet them!
Forgive me . . . I am not often not a man . . .
I am quite well now. . . . Yes, the air . . . the damp.
My window's small—but boasts Aldebaran,
A long hour, late. He's quite the same, Berard,
As when you taught a little boy his name
And pointed to him hanging through the palm trees.
It's very friendly of him to be here. . . .
I almost slipped from prison yesterday.
That was before I knew . . . My evil luck
Was Absalom's: one strand of tell-tale hair
Showed from the wine-butt I was hiding in. . . .
For that attempt I'm being lessoned now
On bread and water—I who was once a king!
Do you remember my first day of battle—
Cased in my golden greaves and coat of mail,
Burnished and proud and brave as seventeen?
He called me then Aldebaran, the prince
Of stars, and was as proud as I, but not
As far, as very far, from doubting tears. . . .

I soldiered well for seventeen: that's something:
And something more that three years afterward

ENZIO'S KINGDOM

I was commander of the imperial armies.
At first it had the zest of sportsmanship
And when we'd meet to plan some new campaign
My heart would swell to know myself his helper.
The best was when we thwarted Gregory.
That was my plan, Berard. To keep the Pope
From holding his great Conclave of the Church,
Or so much of it as was hostile to us,
Seemed of prime urgency, for, once assembled,
We had some glimmering of the onerous outcome.
My father had already sent his letter
To all the Christian kings of Christendom
Protesting 'gainst the Conclave's convocation.
How he and Pietro crackled at its making—
Its scriptural, grandiose air of indignation,
With just enough of formal reverence
To make them swallow down the new wild yeast
Of his rebellious and irreverent scorn.
And when they nominated Gregory
"The Beast with Horns"—and sternly—how we laughed!
It smacked of that audacious mad crusade
He undertook in jest or scorn or malice
And rounded to a cynical success
With wheat and oil and Kamel's tolerant friendship.
Yet in these scornful pranks one could detect
A calculated and subversive purpose:
To mock an idol without retribution
Will jar somewhat the best idolater.
Indeed, I think his mockery's work will last
When much far nobler will have been forgot.
But the letter, though it jarred the Christian kings,

ENZIO'S KINGDOM

Did not prevent the Conclave's call to Rome.
So, as our armies domineered all roads
Converging on the imperial city north
And south, leaving their sole approach by sea,
I offered, half as humorous solution,
To catch the Conclave as it paddled past,
Reeking of lauds and incense, but convoyed
Stoutly enough by the whole fleet of Genoa;
Which done, we'd drop that freightage of old bones—
Three hundred cardinals, archbishops, what-nots—
Into some wholesome dungeon, while the Pope
Would rant and fall to scribbling bulls and banns
At the empty council table. Here was a jest
Fateful, adventurous, that took my father:
Da Vigna too was hopeful: you were absent.
So we devised how I should take the fleet
Of Pisa with what tonnage of our own
I could lay hands to, and strike the Genoese
While sailing down the mainland to the Tiber.
But I remember as our parley ended
My father's ardor wavered and went out,
And he was moody till we were alone.
Then as I turned to leave him he inquired,
"Have you no fear, no secret fear, my son,
Of Rome's much-feared and hard anathema
That falls on you now as it fell on me?"
But all that I could think to answer was,
"I am your son." He gripped me hard at that.
There is some balm in lingering on such moments
When he was proud my bastard blood was his. . . .
Another one was when I dashed from Pisa,
Riding in lathered haste, my tidings' own

ENZIO'S KINGDOM

Glad messenger. Ah, then time's brutal hand
Had not yet brushed the moth-gold from my youth!
Dusty and hollow-eyed and streaked with sweat
I burst upon him with the victory:
Our sally in the dark; the shock at dawn;
How such and such a ship was sunk or boarded;
Where sprang their main resistance, and its toll;
And who their worships were we clapped in prison.
I saved the humor of it for the last.
Archbishop though you are, you too had laughed
At those two prelates pigeon-paunched, red-gilled,
Who started excommunicating me
Right in the face of my own gaping troops.
My father ruffled when I told him of it.
But when I added with what unconcern
I cut in on their curse and whisked them off,
Blowsy with rage, to learn civility
And Christian meekness in a lousy cell—
He laughed till tears were shaking in his beard.
Then a great banquet, jousts and glees and tourneys—
And I the target of his toasts and praises.

There was not much of laughing loud together,
Or banqueting, after the Pisan coup.
Campaigns and sieges, battles and assaults—
Ungilding in the glut and mire of war.
We thought when Gregory died there would be respite,
But wished him back before this Innocent
Had run one scale upon his harp of hate.
He'll likely die now, when his death's no profit.
The evil always die too late for thanks,

Serene and impotent, their worst full blown.
I hated war, but matched against my father's,
My hatred of it was intemperate love.
There never was so great a warrior,
A general so visioned and aggressive,
Who so rebelliously despised his calling.
It wore into his very strength and sinews
Like trace-chains on the haunches of a charger.
But still his camp outlustered any court,
Was rumored into fable as the home
Of every undared dark delirious vice,
And still he browbeat fame and looked the victor. . . .
It was a specious semblance of his world.

When Innocent fled Rome for France, it seemed
Our victory, but was our brink of ruin.
There was no fleet to summon merrily
And catch the Conclave he convened for Lyons.
He did not fall in Gregory's trap. And I
Nor Pietro could devise a scheme to stave
The darkening fate that gathered as we gazed
To hurtle on a head so undeserving.
If he had gone himself, Berard, and stood
Before them in his cloak of burning wrath,
Could they have found him guilty? Oh, I think
They would have swept their croziers up like swords
And sworn to follow him, though bound for hell.
But likely not. They were old tepid men,
By whom to be adjudged as by one's equals
Was desecration and indignity.
So Thaddeus went, and Pietro followed him,
To act the absent and imperial

Protagonist; while one old man and I
With sombre hearts kept near the emperor
And made Turin our waiting place for news.

The tricks of prison life are strange, Berard.
Here in my cell I've paced so many times
That length of hall where his great feast was held
That I can count the casements down one wall,
The lolling torches sconced along the other,
And often, sleepless, in a mad calm dream
I seem to move about there in the moonlight,
Lonesome as Abel's ghost alone in death,
Searching for something missed but unremembered,
And gazing with vague misty eyes far out
Across the night-washed lowlands of Turin.
Why did he choose of all times that for feasting,
Summoning friends, near friends, near enemies,
To drink deep and to make a show of pleasure,
When all the while our hearts were raw with waiting
For news of Thaddeus and his mission's end?
But the room glittered with its crush of guests,
The dipping torch-light through its own blue smoke
Crimsoning carcanets and jewelled clasps,
Daubing with fire the burnished bowls and beakers—
And he too glittered from his daïsed throne
At the long table's end, above the crowd,
Superb in tissued gold and rash abandon.
How wearily for us the mirth rushed on!
And when we heard those clattering hoofs outside
Dash up and halt, how well we knew some fate
With hooded vizor stood, a wall's width from us,
And would not stand there long. So Thaddeus
    entered—

Forgive my telling what you know already!
I am a draft of visions. Hear me out,
Or I shall strangle in their mounting fumes!—
It seemed he'd never walk that length of room
And stand before my father, whispering.
Then lacked the emperor courtesy, if ever:
He brushed the words back Thaddeus was speaking
And rose; the chatter froze away to silence.
His own words sprang across the air like arrows:
"My friends, we have somewhat of news to hear
Which Thaddeus brings still piping from the Pope.
We'll hear it with you. The worst is not too bad
To share with friends, simply, with no concealment.
Speak, Thaddeus, speak: as if to me alone."
And Thaddeus faced us, anguish on his face
And such nobility as heartbreak chisels.

They could find naught wherewith to charge my father
Save heresy—no vileness, no one act
Infamous or diseased with evil outcome!
But day by day they clustered in their church,
Stinking with sweat and incense, and pawed through
The jewelled details of his passionate life,
Seeking for filth, hungry for carrion—
Carrion-beaked and carrion-clawed themselves!
As Thaddeus spoke, I saw those cardinals,
Archbishops, abbots, royal emissaries,
Ranged in the tainted darkness of their church,
Posturing as the world's high court of justice
And tottering through the motions of a trial
Whose sentence had been writ before its charge.

ENZIO'S KINGDOM

Guzzlers and sycophants of envious Rome!
Louis of France, for all his saintliness,
Pled for the emperor, and England's voice
Was just though weak. So potent was the suasion
Of Thaddeus when at last they gave him leave
To answer and defend, the council shook,
They say, with conscience-stabbed irresolution. . . .
But Innocent poured out his eloquent hate
And while the organ groaned, the hymns surged up—
As through some fissure cracked in noisy hell—
Those old men dashed their writhing torches down
And in the awful darkness cursed my father. . . .
'Twas here you will recall that Thaddeus stopped,
Sank to his seat and dumbly clutched the table.
And my father's voice leaped out, "Go on, go on!
The sentence?" It was not Thaddeus who answered.
Da Vigna spoke, standing far down the room,
A late arrival here as at the Conclave:
His tones, clear always, never seemed so clear:
"Anathema and Excommunication."
I saw my father smile. Da Vigna saw it.
He paused and spoke again: "And this besides:
The Holy Roman Empire's Emperor,
Frederick, called the Second, is hereby
Deposed—allegiance to him voided, nay,
Forbidden: thus saith the Conclave with one voice."
Lightning—that blinded as it crashed, downward!
There was a deadly daze of silence. It grew.
All gazed toward my father. But he was silent,
And motionless upon the conspicuous throne.
Their stupor turned ferocious restlessness:
Fear that he searched in vain for words to feed them

ENZIO'S KINGDOM

Smothered my heart and twitched about my nostrils.
But still he did not speak or lift his eyes.
Suddenly swirled the blade-hiss of his voice:
"Arabs, ho there! Fetch here my treasure chests!"
Our wonder was a terror and a stillness
The whole while that they found and brought the
    chests.
We leaned and saw them by the lowest step
And barely let our eyes seek up to where
He sat and gazed upon them. Then he stood,
And slowly step by step came down—stooping,
Horribly focussed on the treasure chests.
One hand trailed to his girdle's keys and hung,
And he himself unlocked and opened each.
He lifted one by one his sacred crowns,
Jerusalem's, the Kingdom's, last the Empire's,
And held them to the light with fixed filmed eyes,
Then strained about to face us, stealthily.
The spectre of his voice called through a cave:
"They are all here." That hollow sound awoke him:
He straightened, set the great crown on his head,
And mounted to his throne the way he would,
All emperor, of world and self possessed.

How hot then poured his lava eloquence,
Molten and vehement! but back of it
Cold mind, and crafty watching of his hearers.
He probed the vacillant world in probing them—
Those faces brutal, unintelligent,
Ferocious in their avidness to live,
Confused or terrified at Pietro's news.
They listened to his wrath. But at his warning

ENZIO'S KINGDOM

Of what submission to such arrogance
Boded to them who were themselves enthroned
And could by this same precedent be dashed
From their high stations at an old man's whim—
He set them breathing hard and fingering sword-hilts.
Then it was pitiful, Berard, to see him,
Warmed at their warming, hope to flush their hearts
With the wild rosy splendor of his dream.
He dignified them with the truth—explained
His kingdom of the spirit for the few,
His fancied freedom for the falcon-souled—
As if they could partake of visioning.
They chilled: and slipped vague glances at their neighbors.
And then I caught da Vigna watching them,
The hovering wings of his eyes gray as old ice.
He felt their ebb of ardor, but no sooner
Than Frederick himself, who forthwith changed
And spiced his argument to suit their stomachs.
He challenged Innocent to pull him down,
Dared him to set another in his place,
Swearing he'd hold it as his sacred right
Though old men cursed and quenched their torches out.
Their strength was equal to a torch's quenching,
But not to quenching an imperial sun.
Then on from there of strengths and weaknesses—
The man-power his from Etna to the Rhine,
His fleets, allies, resources, endless treasure
Against the starveling papal regiments,
The flight from Rome, the general disaffection,
The iterated and unanswered calls

ENZIO'S KINGDOM

For tithes and tribute. Conclaves could convene,
But Victory crowned the strong, and who as strong
In all the armored world as Frederick?
Cheeks flushed and flashing eyes were everywhere:
The hot contagion of his words as always
Had done its work: his last phrase thundering still,
They clashed their swords down on the reeling table,
Tossed up their goblets in a mighty toast,
And shouted, "Death to Rome! Frederick! Frederick!"
He gravely bowed and gravely waved them out
With "Gentlemen, be your sleep calm as mine."

They joined the darkness. With the last one's exit
He sank back in his throne: I kept my place
And waited for his eyes to look for mine.
We were alone: the shadowy hall was empty,
Bleak with disorder, stale with feasting done.
He sat immobile as a carven king:
I feared to rouse him from that fell abstraction
And he seemed not to know I even lived.
The lights waned and the moonlight grew and lengthened
And bars of hollow silver spanned the gloom.
And still we sat apart and no word spoken.
Then I crept down the table to his throne
And stood beneath him, saw his eyes wide open,
But not the eyes I knew. They did not see me.
I mounted one by one the purple steps
And coming to his feet sat there, and leaned
My head against the throne, flush with his knee.

At last I questioned: "What does it mean, my
    father?"
I thought he had not heard me; then he spoke
From loneliness, across an infinite chasm:
"The end. Darkness ahead. Darkness ahead."—
Words the fewest and most sorrowful
That ever sunk their anchors in my soul!
We were so close! yet I could not reach out
And soothe the grief of his profound despair.
The vultures tear us on our several hills
Which neighbor no two closelier than yields
A perfect view of our most loved one's anguish.
I knew he saw the conclave's condemnation
As the immitigable blow of fate
That crashed down all the fabric of his life
And left his hopes dispowered as a dream.
And I knew what he saw was very truth
Though what I saw was only curling chaos
And nothing clear and nothing of fair promise.
So through the ebbing smoke-drifts of the room
I looked out on the lowlands and the moonlight
And watched the ravelled cloud-banks floating past,
The spindrift of a sunset's storm of color,
And thought of his cloud-splendor now so
    toppled. . . .
There was much time for many thoughts to stumble
Before he stirred and spoke in that far way,
But now his voice was frayed and slow with pain:
"Save yourself, Enzio. For you there's time.
You are not safe with Helios any more."
My throat swelled suddenly and all my will
Was in the forcing of a voice to answer:

ENZIO'S KINGDOM

"I will not leave you now; nor ever leave you.
We will fight on as we have fought, together."
His body's quiver was a long time dying:
"We will fight on then, Enzio, my son."
His hand blessed for a moment my bent head.
The torches guttered out; down the long hall,
Across the litter of the banquet table,
The windows poured their caverns of gray fire;
And still he sat, sagged forward, hands on knees,
The imperial crown a red slur round his forehead.
A moon misshapen stumbled down the sky,
Bloody and sick. And there was no more to say. . . .

Another man had broken: not my father.
He fought on, with a difference that grew. . . .
How do we hate iniquity and thrive,
But, hating them that are iniquitous,
Harden and grow ourselves somehow attaint
With the venom hoarded for the unrighteous foe?
Unjust dilemma! We cannot grip an evil
Fleshless, abstract, not cased in him or her
On whom we may lay hands of wrath and ruin!
To not hate wrong rubs out man's one distinction:
Ably to hate it saps the root of reason.
He grew to hate, a clenched, vein-jutting hatred,
And Innocent and them opposed he hated.
The priests will write it in their manuscripts—
For flourish to his catalogue of crimes—
That he was cruel. I have found all men so.
But true it is he hardened after Lyons:
He did not lag in cruelty; indeed,
His old Sicilian temperateness dried up.

ENZIO'S KINGDOM

The tide was set against him: each new day
Brought new defections, losses, perjured friends,
But still he dominated with his dripping sword
The whole peninsula—and for his camp
Built him a city—"Victory," alas.
That monster citadel he meant as answer,
Insult and challenge to the Conclave's edict.
He could not name its name even to me
Afterwards. Verily, Parma, I could wish
To live, if life of mine could work revenge!
It had not fallen, had I not been elsewhere.
Berard, it is not all the treasure lost,
The scoffing of the world, even the death
Of Thaddeus torn, still living, limb from limb,
That makes so passing pitiful to me
Vittoria's capture. But I am picturing always
His gay return from hunting through the woods.
He was so great a hunter, and its love
Medicined him when most his soul was sickened.
I see him, rested by his weariness,
Riding ahead upon his sweating stallion
With all the rough loud hunters in his wake,
And coming to a clearing on the hillside,
And catching sight below him on the plain
Of acred flames where once Vittoria spread
And running ants that were his armies once.
Humiliation heaped on helplessness!
He never hunted after that, Berard,
And lacked, I know, the sweetening of that
Forgetful wholesomeness. That Parma stole.

Deposed, his honor gone, and Thaddeus slain,
There seemed no residue of misery

ENZIO'S KINGDOM

That he need blench at. Yet the worst impended.
This incarnator of uncarnate dreams
Had left for fate to pierce only his heart,
And men had thought that was invulnerable.
Men thought so: we knew better. But your eyes
Were spared the sight of it red-riven, smoking—
Would mine had been! They'd have less fear of sleep
Had not his sickness called me to Cremona.
He ailed, and none could find the seat of ailment,
So he exchanged a captive we had got
Of Parma for Pietro's own physician who
Was there, a prisoner—the mutual gift
Made at da Vigna's counsel, nay, his urgence.
I had not seen him since he spoke so clearly.
He'd been too late to speak out at the Conclave,
But heard the sentence, with some horror doubtless.
When his physician came and saw my father
Feeble with fever, twitching on the bedclothes,
Da Vigna was solicitous, but asked
Leave to depart the city that same day
About the empire's business. Leave was granted,
For I was there to act in his behalf.
When he had gone, and with him the physician
To brew a sleeping potion for the night,
An Arab burst into the room, tottered,
Fell at my father's bedside, gripped his shoulder,
And while swift tears of misery smeared his cheeks
Whispered in Arabic some broken message.
My father roused up with a choking cry,
Struck him across the face, and as he fell
Called for the guards to gag him and imprison;
Then fell back on his bed, sweat-cold and shaking.

ENZIO'S KINGDOM

"Let not da Vigna leave tonight," he gasped.
"Be here with him at dark, and nothing said."
The night came soon, though slowlier than night comes,
And found da Vigna, me, the Arab guards
Assembled in his chamber. It reeked of fever.
But, saying that his health was mended somewhat,
He sat half-dressed, though haggard as I thought,
And calm, except his eyes, blue-bright, unpausing.
Beside him was a table with his papers,
A rush-light, and his ruby-hilted broad-sword.
He was midway in giving us instructions
As to provisioning the eastern army,
When Pietro's good physician padded in,
His hands about a bowl of sleeping draught.
My father smiled: "All sleep is good, but one
Is best. You mean me well?" "Master, with this,"
The leech replied, "you will sleep well till morning."
"Which will break, doubtless, with a trumpet blast,"
My father sneered. "'Twill take as much to sain me."
Then carelessly to Pietro, "We can trust him?"
Who was as careless in his clear-voiced answer,
"My life is almost hourly in his hands:
I've never found a cause to think him faithless."
My father's snake-arm struck and bit his sword-hilt,
His voice snarled through his nostrils at the leech:
"Then drink it half yourself." The man shrank back,
Sick-green and speechless, horrible with fear.
The drink splashed in his hands, had fallen but
My father clutched it up half-full and called,
"Bring now the prisoner that prays for sleep,"
And instantly from some near room there walked

A blank-eyed prisoner between two Arabs.
My father held the bowl to him and said,
"Drink this, my friend; my hope is you will sleep."
The man said not a word, but drank it down.
"Sirs," my father turned to us, "sit down.
There's patient waiting here for all of us."
So we sat down; the man, too, that had drunk.
Bound in a common cataleptic coil,
Speechless, transfixed, we watched his poor meek face—
Our separate terrors wrestling with our wills
To burst out in a scream and break the nightmare.
At last his eyelids flickered, lowered, closed.
Our senses strained, each one an ear, to catch
The rustle of his breathing. His body slackened,
Wavered and lurched, and toppled to the floor.
He lay there twisted, still, so unreposeful
One longed to make him easy, but none stirred.
And our own spell of hideous quietude
Seemed part of his eternal sprawled discomfort.
The emperor broke it with a voice as dead
As were his eyes and they were tombs: "Pietro,
Lean down and lay your head upon his heart
And tell me if it beats." And Pietro reeled
And sounds clawed in his throat and choked away
And all his body wrinkled back with horror.
But he knelt down and leaned and pressed his ear
Upon the spot where that man's heart had beat.
His eyes grew wide and wider, no more wings
Hovering, then they shut, and when his voice
Rasped through an opening in his throat, it had
No old-time clearness. "It beats no more," he said.

ENZIO'S KINGDOM

The emperor staggered—thunder might have struck him,
Instead of words just heard. He took one step,
Lunged through the leech's body with his sword,
Who belched up blood, crumpled and fell, stone dead.
The smoking huddle lay across his feet—
He spurned it off and spoke: "Take out the dung."
Then tottered, stayed him on his bleeding sword,
And closed his eyes, and held his hand upon them,
As if gone blind of infinite despair,
But opened them and plunged them into Pietro's
And held them there, as though for all his grief
There must be comfort in those once friendly depths.
But Pietro flung himself face down and clasped
His feet and cried, "Pardon, Imperial Master,
Pardon!" The sword dropped from my father's hand
And both his hands groped upward to his throat
And worried there and tore his collar back:
His eyes closed in their hollows, his features worked.
He strangled so before he could groan out:
"Another word—not that—another word!"
And then his reason reeled and stumbled back,
Calling one word as if there were no other:
"Confessed, confessed, confessed, confessed—O God!"
Da Vigna crushed his face against his arm,
Shuddered, then lay quite still, so did not see
The emperor stoop above him, gaze, recoil,
And draw his foot back with a snarl of loathing.
Berard, Berard, I would forget his change
From agony to rage and hate, though just!
He said no more than it was true to say,
Pouring the words like acid over Pietro,

ENZIO'S KINGDOM

Words you can guess, deserved—oh, well deserved—
And yet, when heard, unworthy of my father.
Let me not think of that! O God! O God!
I shrank from him, he did not seem my father,
But some gross beast that had gone beastly mad—
His flaccid mouth too weak to hold its water,
And all his face a pouch of flesh that glistened!
And, oh, the beastly cry that ended it:
"Burn out his eyes and bind him to a mule
And drive him, socket-empty, through the world—
An epigram of Frederick's love turned hate!" . . .
Justice, indeed, but who is ripe for justice?
Pietro had fainted when the Arabs touched him.
The emperor watched him heaved out like a corpse,
Then blindly motioned us to leave the room—
And I left gladly, left him palsied, shrunken;
So even I was dimmed with treachery
And let my spirit falter in its love.

My bed was in a chamber close to his,
A bed that night no sleep had tucked and pillowed.
I lay and killed the horror in my soul,
And reckoned up his measureless misery.
I saw what I had never seen before,
That he was young no longer. He had looked
Almost an old man when they lifted Pietro—
Slack and uncertain, creased and gray with strain.
I had not thought he'd ever not be hale
Or wear the taint of time in any crevice.
Not death, but mind and body's stealthy crumble
Before they slough and fall is nature's worst.
And nothing twitches so the heart as seeing

[134]

ENZIO'S KINGDOM

In one we love the wall's first visible crack.
I wept for him, Berard, and as I wept
His great voice suddenly burst across the stillness
And he was calling, "Enzio, Enzio, Enzio!"
As hell's poor damned must call on their first night.
I rushed into his chamber. He was sitting
Upon the bedside, clutching it for prop,
His mighty shoulders stooping, and his head
Bowed on his breast. I ran to him, dropped down,
And saw his eyes—my father's eyes, Berard!—
Smoking with terror! He seized my hands, my arms,
Felt up my face, across my hair—oh, blindly—
Whispering "Is it you, Enzio? Is it you?"
I slipped my arm around him, steadied him.
But still he shook, and whispered huskily:
"He knew me. My heart lay beating in his hand.
He was the faithful Peter of our Kingdom.
He did not hate me: could he love, he loved me;
But he was overborne by the turned tide.
There was no anchor to his intellect:
Truth he saw, but could not hook its grapples
Under his heart. The long time that I prospered,
Their outcry moved him not: but at the end
The universal condemnation shook him,
And when the filthy world cried out 'Unclean'
He could not feel me clean, although he knew it,
So slackened in his faith, doubting, doubting,
And at my ebb of fortune did—what he did!
If Pietro can desert me, who will stay?
If he can be untrue, where look for faith?
There're daggers in each doorway, in each aisle
Spears, and each window has drawn arrows. Oh,

ENZIO'S KINGDOM

No cup but reeks with poison and no heart
But rears with viper hate and treachery!
No way to turn—no going back or forward—
And none to wade the blood and darkness with me!
Enzio, Enzio, we are alone, and you—
Will you be going too? Will you? Will you?
The way I walk leads to a ghastly nowhere,
But, oh, beseech you, leave me not alone!
Be pitiful, for all the love I bear you—
My son, my son!''
Berard, the noblest of all emperors
Lay sobbing in my arms like some poor child,
And I was healing him of dreadful tears
With words my own would hardly let me utter—
Mere words, though weak in wisdom, strong in love.
No night of mine can ever be as choked
With misery and helplessness again.

So wounded mortally, he still could live
Because I clove to him. Then I was taken. . . .
All that his son could do I did in that
Last battle: more than any but his son
Could dream of doing. The Modanese betrayed us.
There was no help. Their dead lay tiered around me
And ours had left me friendless by the evening.
I could not tell my blood from blood I'd emptied
And I had fainted when they captured me.
There was no help. Fate meant to break him so
With the one cruelty unused, but hoarded.
I knew he threatened and implored, and vainly,
For I was brag and safeguard of Bologna:
Assaulted, she would tear me limb from limb

ENZIO'S KINGDOM

Before his maddened eyes, and there's not gold
Sufficient in the earth to ransom me.
And, after that, I knew he could not stay
And fight the fight out in the north alone,
But would drag back like some great wounded beast
Into the Kingdom's lair and sanctuary. . . .
Yet, all his heart was homesick for had gone,
Vanished in cloud-dust, dust of death, or prison:
His kingdom was a boundary, bounding nothing.
He died because he had no heart to live:
Life was unworthy of his presence in it. . . .
I'm glad he died away from the loud world,
With twilight woods around him, in your arms;
And glad his mind was steady to the end
And he knew Death. . . . It was a kingly meeting—
Death and my father. . . . You say he had his bed
Borne to that window of the hunting lodge
That faces west, and lay there open-eyed,
In some great revery beyond your ken,
Watching the wintry sunset winnow out
From red to gray behind the keen still trees;
And then his eyes called to you and you stooped,
And heard his words, but two: "Tell Enzio."
He closed his lids, regretless that no strength
Would open them again. . . . When he walked
   through
The portals of Death's purple-raftered house,
I know the other guests arose and stood. . . .

My words have bridged the two walls of the night.
The far one crumbles now. . . . Come, look, Berard.
Aldebaran has gone with his companions.

[137]

ENZIO'S KINGDOM

An old moon, blue with cold, limps up the east,
Thin as the new. He will be overtaken,
And halfway up his mountain die, in the sun . . .
A beggar's death . . . an old man's death, alone. . . .
Old age which should be but a hill's descent,
May be an ever-upward mountain toil,
By night, through empty cold, in loneliness. . . .
By count, Berard, my years are thirty: but
My living days ahead are all old age.
Here is a crass unthoughtedness, a waste,
A mere continuing that is not life,
Miserable to me, to no man helpful. . . .
Our utmost is a stave of noble song
Scrawled blindly on the scrap of page allowed
And tossed into the sea—unlearned, unpraised,
Of no avail. Yet it could be ignoble:
I'll not have mine default in fortitude
By ending it. I'll let the stave be rounded,
As if my father were my listener. . . .

I cannot see by what integrity
High Heaven annihilated so his efforts!
Unless there be no heaven—and that I'll grant
Sooner than that his vision's fate was just! . . .
A vision's own validity and worth
Has no transmuting power to turn it facts;
And, even turned, with all the needed aid
Of accident combined with dominant will,
Its best escapes: its second best may live
And for a dubious cycle shed its lustre.
But his was buttressed by all things save chance,

ENZIO'S KINGDOM

And there's no tatter left, no single gleam.
What hope for this wrong world if such things be?
We are so hemmed by horror, pressed by darkness,
That there's no lighted calm where we may pause
And see our evil destinies in bulk—
Bathed in an awful loveliness, perhaps,
And part of some transcending glimpsed coherence.
There is no certain thing I can lay hold on
And say, "This, this is good! This will I worship!"
Except my father. For he intended like
A god: or, since I see no signs of gods,
If some day earth shall house divinities
In guise of men, or in some guise I guess not,
They shall be minded, willed, and souled like him.
And so despite life's infamy and failure
I thank whatever may be thanked that I
Was heaved up from the insentient void and saw
In him divinity, though marred and baffled.
It seems now nothing else in life was worth
The seeing. What the crop is of his sowing
I am not seer enough to speculate:
I only know the grain was golden and
The earth is culpable if there's no harvest. . . .
Darkness; darkness; and for me no hope
Of any light, unless there be some place
For tarrying, where he will tarry for me.

Now let me kneel, old man, and clasp your knees
And bend my head the way I learned when little,
And you will bless me through your falling tears. . . .
Ah, you and I are all that now remain
Of his heart's Kingdom, so we must keep worthy. . . .
Go now, Berard. The waiting's empty, but
The end is sure, and we have much to dream on.

EPILOGUE

This wind upon my mouth, these stars I see,
The breathing of the night above the trees,
Not these nor anything my senses touch
Are real to me or worth the boon of breath.
But all the never-heard, the never-seen,
The just-beyond my hands can never reach,
These have a substance that is stout and sure,
These brace the unsubstantial sliding world,
And lend the evanescent actual
An air of life, a tint of worth and meaning.
Shall dust, fortuitously blown into
A curve of moon or leaf or throat or petal
And seeding back to vacancy and dust,
Content my soul with its illiterate
And lapsing loveliness? Or tired knowledge
Make credible the hard decree of living?
Oh, I have heard a golden trumpet blowing
Under the night. Another warmth than blood
Has coursed, though briefly, through my intricate veins.
Some sky is in my breast where swings a hawk
Intemperate for immortalities
And unpersuaded by the show of death.
I am content with that I cannot prove.

Made in the USA
Columbia, SC
10 February 2019